Improving schools and governing bodies

School improvement is currently at the top of both the educational and political agendas. The most recent Education Acts have given school governing bodies very considerable powers and responsibilities, and they are increasingly being asked to work together with the headteacher on improving standards in their schools. This means that there is a real need for texts that aim to support governors in their new role.

This book seeks to provide a framework for governors who wish to work most effectively at raising standards in their schools. It is based on substantial research carried out in the field but it also gives the necessary practical guidance. Examples are given of how governing bodies are contributing to improvement in a wide variety of schools and how they are helping to set targets, and to monitor and evaluate progress. Other areas looked at include their role as a link between the school, the parents and the wider community, and their function both during and after OFSTED inspections.

Good governors are proactive rather than reactive, and they can contribute significantly to a school's success. This book will provide school governors and senior staff with a blueprint for working together effectively to bring about positive change in their schools.

Michael Creese was formerly a headteacher and an LEA governor training co-ordinator. He is currently using his expertise as a freelance educational consultant, researcher and writer. **Peter Earley** has published extensively in this field and is currently a senior lecturer at the Institute of Education, University of London.

Improving schools and governing bodies

Making a difference

Michael Creese and
Peter Earley

London and New York

First published 1999
by Routledge
11 New Fetter Lane, London EC4P 4EE

Simultaneously published in the USA and Canada
by Routledge
29 West 35th Street, New York, NY 10001

Routledge is an imprint of the Taylor & Francis Group

© 1999 Michael Creese and Peter Earley

Typeset in Goudy by Routledge
Printed and bound in Great Britain by MPG Books Ltd, Bodmin

British Library Cataloguing in Publication Data
A catalogue record for this book is available from the British
Library

Library of Congress Cataloging-in-Publication Data
Creese, Michael.
Improving schools and governing bodies: making a
difference/Michael Creese and Peter Earley.
p. cm.
Includes bibliographical references and index.
1. School improvement programs – Great Britain. 2. School boards
– Great Britain. I. Earley, Peter. II. Title.
LB2822.84.G7C75 1999   99-20332
371.2'00941 – dc21   CIP

ISBN 0-415-20510-7 (hbk)
ISBN 0-415-20511-5 (pbk)

Contents

Figures

Foreword

I am delighted to be able to contribute a foreword to this important book. *Improving Schools and Governing Bodies* is important in many ways, but let me comment briefly on three of its qualities.

First, through analysis and case study the book marks a new level of maturity and insight into the role of the governing body. Key to this is the emphasis on establishing the right climate for improvement, and the governors' contribution to this endeavour is carefully articulated. Second, the book offers a sensitive appraisal of the head's task in creating the appropriate environment in which governors can most effectively carry out their role. The synergy achieved through the active partnership between governor and head is well documented. Third, and for me most excitingly, the book conceptualises the governors' role within the school improvement framework. The core mission of the school is seen to be high-quality teaching and learning, and it is this that above all informs the work of both governor and head.

Michael Creese and Peter Earley are ideally suited to author this book. They have been influential in governor training and research over a decade, and the benefits of this experience are clearly demonstrated in the pages that follow. In the book they have deftly blended narrative, research, analysis and case study in a way that powerfully illuminates their key themes. In this way the book provides not only a worthy addition to the literature on governing bodies, but also to that on school improvement.

My current favourite educational aphorism is attributed to Lawrence Downey – 'that a school teaches in three ways: by what it teaches, by how it teaches and the kind of place it is'. In *Improving Schools and Governing Bodies* Michael Creese and Peter Earley illustrate in an acute and practical way how the partnership between governors and head can make this ideal a reality.

Professor David Hopkins
Chair of the School of Education
Dean of Education, Nottingham University
December 1998

Acknowledgements

First and foremost, we are delighted to have the opportunity to express our gratitude publicly to the governors, headteachers, teachers and pupils of all of the schools in which we worked. We were met everywhere with kindness and consideration, and invited to share fully in what were, on occasion, rather difficult moments in the lives of their schools. Without their encouragement and support, this book could not have been written.

Second, we are grateful to those who sponsored our researches. The Cambridge-based pilot project was funded jointly by Royal Mail and the School of Education. The subsequent substantive study was funded by BT, Royal Mail, Unilever and the School of Education. The London project was part funded by the Institute of Education, University of London and Oxford Brookes University.

We are grateful to Lawrie Baker for his contribution to the fieldwork in the London-based project, to Howard Bradley OBE, the former director of the Cambridge Institute of Education for his involvement in, and support of, the pilot project and to Professor Donald McIntyre of the School of Education, University of Cambridge for his encouragement and advice during the main Cambridge project.

Finally, we wish to express our thanks to Professor David Hopkins of Nottingham University for finding the time in a very busy schedule to write the Foreword to our book.

Abbreviations

A level	Advanced level
AGIT	Action for Governors' Information and Training
BIS	Banking Information Services
DES	Department of Education and Science
DFE	Department for Education
DfEE	Department for Education and Employment
GCSE	General Certificate of Secondary Education
GM	Grant-Maintained
GNVQ	General National Vocational Qualification
GTC	Governor Training Co-ordinator
HMI	Her Majesty's Inspectors (of Schools)
ICT	Information and Communication Technology
INSET	Inservice Education and Training
IQEA	Improving the Quality of Education for All project
ISCG	Institution for School and College Governors
ISIP	International School Improvement Project
LEA	Local Education Authority
LMS	Local Management of Schools
MBA	Master of Business Administration
OCEA	Oxford Consortium for Educational Achievement
OFSTED	Office for Standards in Education
PANDAs	Performance and Assessment Reports
PTA	Parent–Teacher Association
QCA	Qualifications and Curriculum Authority
SATs	Standard Assessment Tasks
SDP	School Development Plan
SEN	Special Educational Needs
SENCO	Special Educational Needs Co-ordinator
SIP	School Improvement Plan
SMT	School Management Team
STRB	School Teachers' Review Body
SWOT	Strengths, Weaknesses, Opportunities and Threats

Introduction

Those who become school governors must sometimes wonder why they volunteered! Perhaps they had a child already in the school, an interest in education in general or maybe they were invited to join the governing body because they possess skills that the other governors thought would be useful. Whatever the reason, we hope that above all school governors want to make a difference – to make their schools better. We believe that it is no accident that first on the list of governors' responsibilities in *School Governors: A Guide to the Law* is 'deciding (with the head and the local education authority (LEA) if appropriate) the aims and policies of the school and *how the standards of education can be improved*' (DfEE 1997a: 15, our italics). School improvement, however, is about more than simply getting better examination results, important though that is, and, in any case, it may not be easy at first sight to see how governors can contribute to the raising of standards when they are not actually teaching the pupils.

In this book we aim to show you how governors, in a very wide variety of situations, have helped their schools to improve and have contributed to the development of a climate that encourages improvement. It is based on data gathered during two research projects, one based at the School of Education, Cambridge University and the other at the Institute of Education, University of London. Brief details of the twenty-three schools involved in the two studies are included in the Appendix. We do not claim to have studied a representative sample of governing bodies but, taking the two projects together, a very wide variety of schools, in very differing settings and situations, has been covered. We were seeking to learn about and share good practice and, with limited resources, we therefore confined our study to those schools in which governors appeared to be making an important contribution to improvement. However, we do believe that the study of good practice offers valuable insights into governance in general.

The Cambridge project arose initially from discussions during a series of courses for governors and headteachers/senior managers under the title 'Managing the Effective School'. The question arose of how governors could contribute to improvement within their schools – how they could 'make a difference'. In the summer of 1996, Michael Creese and Howard Bradley under-took a pilot project funded jointly by the School of Education's Development Fund and Royal Mail (Creese and Bradley 1997) during which they interviewed the headteacher and chair of governors together in seven schools – primary, secondary and special – across East Anglia. As a result of this pilot project, funding (from the Development Fund, BT, Royal Mail and Unilever) was gained for a more substantive study. This involved the writing of case studies, over a two-year period, on the work of sixteen governing bodies – in primary, secondary and special schools in six LEAs. Three of the schools were grant-maintained and two were on the list of schools 'in need of special measures to improve'. By the time that this project began, Howard Bradley had retired and the fieldwork was undertaken by Michael Creese. The circumstances of the sixteen schools varied widely but they all had one thing in common; the gover-nors and staff together were committed to improvement and the schools were chosen for study on that basis. Data were collected mainly through interviews and by observing meetings of various types; occasionally these were meetings of the full governing body but more frequently they were subgroups of the governing body. Across the sixteen schools, ninety-six individual governors and members of staff were interviewed (a few of them by telephone) and fifty-eight meetings of various groups were attended. Governors were observed under-taking a wide range of activities including interviewing candidates for a deputy headship, negotiating the headteacher's salary, visiting classrooms and meeting pupils and their parents. Appropriate documentation was also studied. Once all of the relevant data had been collected at a school, a draft case study report was then written for that school and copies of this were sent to the school for distri-bution to the key informants for comment and possible amendment, though, in the event, very few amendments were forthcoming. A list of specific points of particular interest was included at the end of each individual case study report and a list of these covering all sixteen schools was drawn up, which enabled a number of emerging themes and common factors to be identified.

The study based at the Institute of Education, University of London was smaller in scale. It began at Oxford Brookes University and lasted for two years. It attempted to build upon the author's earlier work (Earley 1994) and aimed to focus on schools and governing bodies that were 'making a difference'. There is a growing body of research that shows that schools in disadvantaged and deprived locations are less able to recruit governors or to find governors with the necessary skills and expertise that schools require. For this reason the research was carried out in schools in less advantaged locations. The aim was to demonstrate that governing bodies could operate effectively 'against the odds' and that effective governing bodies were not only found in 'the leafy suburbs'. Seven schools (four primary, one middle and two secondary) were selected in four LEAs. The selections were made by the LEA Governor Training Co-ordi-nators (GTCs) who were asked to choose schools that were not generally considered to be in favourable circumstances but that, in their view, had an effective governing body. Effectiveness was defined broadly but particularly in terms of the governing body's key role in raising standards and contributing to a climate of improvement. The principal aim of the research was to ascertain how governing bodies contributed to school improvement.

The research project commenced by interviewing twelve LEA GTCs. From these interviews four LEAs were selected and the respective GTCs asked to give consideration to possible case studies. A total of seven governing bodies were identified and all agreed to be involved in the project. The research was primarily interview-based with interviews undertaken with headteachers, chairs and governors. Face to face interviews were undertaken with the heads and the chairs of governors separately, and with the head and chair together. In addition, telephone interviews were conducted with four governors (one of each governor category) from each of the seven schools. A total of forty-two interviews were carried out with heads, chairs and governors.

In the first chapter of this volume we discuss theoretical ideas on school effectiveness and school improvement, offer a definition of improvement and consider the management of change. We look at how governors are contributing to improvement in their schools and, at least as importantly, how they are helping to foster a climate and a culture in which improvement flourishes. In Chapter 2 we consider the link between effectiveness and efficiency; effective governing bodies are efficient in that they conduct their business in such a way as to enable them to deal properly with the big issues. Almost all governing bodies now operate a system of committees and subgroups but this brings the possibility of some governors feeling excluded from the major decisions and perhaps the growth of an 'A-team' and a 'B-team' on the governing body. In subsequent chapters we consider, in more detail, governors' involvement in a range of activities that contribute to improvement, illustrating these with vignettes from the schools in our studies. We hope that governors will find these practical illustrations helpful and we are happy to acknowledge that we have taken this idea from *Schools at the Centre? A Study of Decentralisation* by Bullock and Thomas (1997). In order to help the reader who may be unfamiliar with some of the acronyms used in education, we have included a glossary of those used in the text.

We hope the ideas included in this book will be of use to governors, governor trainers, headteachers and other members of staff, particularly those preparing for headship. Readers should remember, however, that all governing bodies and all schools are different and that what works for one group of governors in one school will not necessarily be immediately transferable to a different situation. Above all, a strong sense of partnership between the governors and the staff, between lay people and the professionals, is crucial. This means that there will be a shared sense of purpose, a clear vision of where the school is heading and an understanding of the respective roles of governors and staff.

Chapter 1

Making a difference
Effectiveness and improvement

We have to believe that we can make a difference.

(Primary school governor)

Introduction

Being effective means having an effect – making a difference. Research tells us that some schools are more effective than others, i.e. that pupils attending those schools achieve more than pupils attending apparently similar schools. Research also identifies factors that appear to be common to these effective schools. There has been less research into the effectiveness of governing bodies, but what there has been suggests that governing bodies also vary in their effectiveness. However, governors generally want to do a job that is worthwhile and are much more likely to remain on the governing body if they feel that they have a role to play in making a difference. 'When the governors and head are engaging with the quality issues that matter for the school, such active participation generates positive feelings for all who work there' (Holt and Hinds 1994: 17).

In recent years interest has shifted from trying to identify the factors that contribute to school effectiveness to attempting to understand how schools may be helped to improve, i.e. how to become more effective. No matter how effective a school or a governing body may be, there is always room for improvement. The notion of 'continuous improvement' – best summarised by the phrase 'you don't have to be ill to get better' – is one that underpins the drive for school improvement. The standard of the pupils' work in one or more subject areas may be significantly below that in other aspects of the curriculum or there may be weaknesses in some aspect of the cross-curricular work, including of course the non-academic work of the school. Governing bodies can improve in the sense that they can become more efficient and more effective in helping their schools to improve.

Effective schools

> An effective school can be defined as one in which the pupils progress further than might be predicted from considerations of their attainment when they enter the school.
>
> (Mortimore 1991)

School effectiveness is now usually defined in terms of pupil outcomes. Research (e.g. Rutter et al. 1979, Mortimore et al. 1988, Sammons et al. 1995) has shown that the school which a child attends can make a significant difference to her/his performance. The more effective the school the greater the 'value-added' to the pupils' performance, i.e. the greater the pupils' attainments in relation to what might have been expected in the light of their past record. Mortimore points to the significance of the 10 per cent difference in a child's GCSE results that can be made by attendance at a more effective school. Though this variation may appear small it can be the difference that opens up the opportunity of taking A levels and eventual entry into one of the professions. Schools are becoming more skilled in measuring the difference that they make; more reliable and more detailed information (e.g. Qualification and Curriculum Authority (QCA) benchmarking data and Performance and Assessment Reports (PANDAs)) are now becoming available about the performance of their pupils over the years and about the performance of pupils in schools of a similar type (e.g. in catchment area, entitlement to free school meals). Governors and staff together can use this information to set targets for improvement.

How might the effectiveness of a school be judged? The above definition of effectiveness appears to stress academic attainment alone but it might appear foolish to judge a school on only one aspect of its performance. The OFSTED Handbook for Inspections (OFSTED 1994a), well-known to governors and teachers, sets out four criteria by which the overall performance of the school will be judged by the inspectors. These are:

- the standards of achievement;
- the quality of education provided;
- the efficiency with which resources are managed;
- the spiritual, moral, social and cultural development of pupils.

The OFSTED position is that fulfilment of these criteria constitutes effectiveness. A slightly different view is that an effective school is one that maximises the chance of efficient learning taking place in every classroom for every pupil (Reid et al. 1987). If this is the case, what is to be learnt and who decides on this? It may not be easy to arrive at an agreed definition as to precisely what constitutes an effective school; those concerned – pupils, parents, teachers, governors, members of the wider community – may well have differing ideas as to what effectiveness means for them. For some, academic performance alone will be the lodestar, while others may envisage broader objectives covering the whole range of a pupil's development. Schools should attempt to discover through discussion and debate the views held by the principal stakeholders (Harris et al. 1996). For instance, when the governors of one of the secondary schools involved in our research were involved in a strategic planning exercise, they came up with some rather broader objectives than had been suggested by the teachers. The staff and governors together must then decide, in the light of these discussions, what their priorities and goals should be, and communicate these clearly to all. 'Governors, head and staff need some shared understanding of what the school is trying to achieve and how it is going about it' (DES 1991: 13).

Lists of factors found in effective schools have been drawn up by a number of authors (e.g. Sammons et al. 1995). These factors include, for instance, shared vision and goals, purposeful teaching and high expectations of pupils. However, none of the lists makes any explicit reference to the impact of the governing body on the school's effectiveness, though this may be because some, though not all, of the research predates the considerable increase in the powers of governors since 1988. The nearest approach to governors is the recognition that a high degree of parental involvement is present in effective schools. However, From Failure to Success (OFSTED 1997), a report showing how being placed on the register of special measures has helped schools to improve, notes that one of the common characteristics of improving schools is that they have sought means of making their governing bodies more effective. We shall discuss this point further in Chapter 7 which considers the role of the governing body in relation to OFSTED inspections.

The move towards the delegation of control of the school's budget to the governing body through the Local Management of Schools (LMS) scheme or, previously in the case of Grant-Maintained (GM) schools giving the governing body total control, was part of the previous government's programme to raise standards of attainment in schools. 'If the system itself were changed to one of self-governing, self-managing, budget centres, which were obliged for their very survival to respond to the "market", then there would be an in-built mechanism to raise standards' (Sexton 1987: 8–9). These moves, which might have been expected to provide opportunities for governing bodies to have greater influence in the running of their schools have, however, often led to increased power in the hands of the headteacher. For example, Levacic (1995) found in her research that the majority of the governing bodies were operating in the advisory and supportive roles, and that they were in an unequal partnership with the head. Similarly, Shearn and his colleagues (1995a, 1995b) found that in the majority of the schools, the head was essentially in charge with the governors having little impact upon the school's direction. In some cases this was with the approval of the governors and in others it arose by default because the governors were unwilling or unable to take on their new responsibility. In a few cases, the headteacher had out-manoeuvred the governors in order to retain control.

Effective governing bodies

There has been much less research into what constitutes an effective governing body than there has been into the effectiveness of schools. Neither has the link between the effectiveness of the governing body and the effectiveness of the school been clearly demonstrated. 'We cannot assume *a priori* that if a governing body becomes skilled at discharging its responsibilities, this necessarily means that the school becomes more effective or more efficient' (Deem *et al.* 1995: 112).

Governing Bodies and Effective Schools (DFE/BIS/OFSTED 1995) lists the main features of an effective governing body as being:

- working as a team;
- having a good relationship with the headteacher;
- managing time and delegating effectively;
- having effective meetings;
- knowing the school;
- being concerned for their own training and development.

Creese (1995) suggests that, in addition to these, an effective governing body is one which:

- works in partnership with the staff;
- is concerned to promote school improvement;
- forms an effective link between the school and the community.

During inspections of schools carried out during the spring term of 1998, OFSTED inspectors assessed the performance of governing bodies particularly in relation to the performance of their strategic role. Those governing bodies given a good grading were those where the complementary roles of the governors and senior managers were well-defined and evident through good practice; where the governors were highly influential in setting aims and targets for their school and where they identified financial and other priorities, and monitored progress towards achieving them. The inspectors found that the performance of three-quarters of the governing bodies was satisfactory or better, with governors in secondary schools doing slightly better at reviewing progress in their schools than their primary colleagues. One-third of governing bodies were totally reliant upon the information that they received from the headteacher and senior staff as a basis for making their judgements.

Michael Tomlinson, Director of Operations at OFSTED, speaking at a conference for governor trainers in Cardiff in September 1998 stated that the best cases of effective governance found during the survey shared the following characteristics:

- influential heads who responded well to constructive criticism;
- the relationship between governors and staff was well understood by all – especially the staff;
- there was a rigorous approach to the monitoring of standards of education;
- success in reaching present targets was carefully evaluated and challenging targets for the future were set.

One way of considering the performance of a governing body is to assess it on two criteria, the level of support that it gives to the school and the level of challenge that it provides. This is shown in Figure 1.1, which is based on the 'Effective Governing Body Exercise' (Oxfordshire LEA 1998).

Some governing bodies – the abdicators – offer neither support nor challenge to their schools. The supporters' clubs offer a lot of support but little challenge while the adversaries offer little support but challenge the staff at every opportunity. Ideally, the governing body is working in partnership with the staff offering

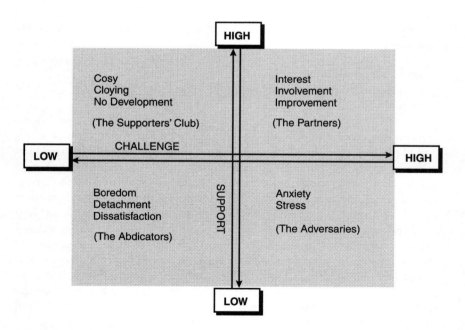

Figure 1.1 **The effective governing body**

a great deal of support but not being afraid to ask the teachers to account for their actions. The four types of governing body may be characterised as follows:

The abdicators

Key phrase: 'We leave it to the professionals.'
These governors claim to be very busy people; they aren't able to get into school as often as they would like. They don't have time to go to training sessions – in any case they believe that it's all common sense really and the money is better spent on books for the children. They believe that they have a good head and leave it all to her/him.

The adversaries

Key phrase: 'We have to keep our head up to the mark.'
These governors visit the school very often, sometimes without warning, and keep a very close eye on all aspects of the work of school. They are frequently very critical of what they see and they seek to make all the decisions about the running of the school.

The supporters' club

Key phrase: 'We're here to support the head.'
These governors have delegated control to the head who takes all the decisions. The governors see their role as offering advice and support. They spend a lot of time discussing the school environment and monitor the school's expenditure very closely. They don't know many of the teachers.

The partners

Key phrase: 'We share everything – good or bad!'
These governors work in partnership with the head and staff, and all have a clear understanding of their respective roles. There is mutual trust and respect. Governors are equal partners in the planning, monitoring and evaluation processes, and they place a premium on both staff and governor development.

It is not easy to estimate how many governing bodies are working in a real partnership with the staff and making a significant difference to the life and work of their schools. Jamieson (quoted in Gann 1998) suggests that around 80 per cent of governing bodies are supporters' clubs, doing not much more than approving the activities of the headteacher and cheering the school on from the sidelines. From his survey of a sample of OFSTED reports, Creese (1997) arrived at a similar figure, suggesting that perhaps only between 5 and 10 per cent of governing bodies are really having a significant impact on the life and work of their schools even though they may see themselves as effective. We need a paradigm shift in the expectations of the governors' role that will enable more governing bodies to make a real contribution to the effectiveness of their schools and this will require a change of attitude on the part of some governors and headteachers.

What do we mean by school improvement?

One of the earliest, and most frequently quoted, definitions of school improvement is that adopted by the International School Improvement Project (ISIP): 'A systematic, sustained effort aimed at change in learning and other related internal conditions in one or more schools, with the ultimate aim of accomplishing educational goals more effectively' (Van Velzen *et al.* 1985: 48). Stoll and Fink (1996) highlight the importance of careful planning, management and continuity even in the face of difficulties, and emphasise the teaching and learning focus of improvement as well as the need for conditions within the organisation that support change.

In *Improving Schools* (OFSTED 1994b) school improvement is defined as the ways in which schools:

- raise standards;
- enhance quality;
- increase efficiency;
- achieve greater success in promoting pupils' spiritual, moral, social and cultural development; in a word the ethos of the school.

We have seen earlier that these are the four areas of a school's work in which performance is judged during an OFSTED inspection. Improvement in one of these categories may well lead, in addition, to improvement elsewhere. For instance, improvement in the school's ethos through the operation of a new behaviour policy might be expected to lead to improved performance by pupils. Similarly, enhancing the quality of the curriculum on offer could well lead to an improvement in standards. Hopkins and his colleagues take a slightly wider view of school improvement, seeing it as 'enhancing student outcomes *as well as* strengthening the school's capacity for managing improving initiatives' (Hopkins *et al.* 1996: 1, their italics). Taking these two definitions together, one might therefore look to find governors contributing to the raising of standards through, for example, their contribution to their school's monitoring and review programme, to increasing efficiency by putting in place energy-saving schemes or enhancing the school's capacity to manage change by using their management experience gained elsewhere. The change will not necessary be large-scale and dramatic. Bradley (1991) suggests that a process of continuous improvement based on a series of relatively small steps may actually have greater long-term benefits than the 'great leap forward'.

For example, the governors of a primary school became involved in what might appear as a relatively small-scale project when their Site and Environment Group took on a playground improvement project. The school had the traditional, large, open, tarmac playground on which the children play at break and lunchtime. This area was, by its very nature, rather stark and its use tended to be dominated by games of football, leaving little space for other activities and also causing a number of minor accidents.

There was general concern amongst parents, governors and staff about the security of the school and playground. Bullying and pupil behaviour were also issues that had attracted attention nationally and the staff were developing a new behaviour policy, although there were very few instances of bullying in the school. As part of the development process, a questionnaire was given to the pupils and they were asked to identify areas of the playground in which they felt insecure. There was a desire on the part of the headteacher and staff that 'play should be a learning experience for the pupils in which they were able to develop a range of skills' (headteacher). The project achieved a number of results including fencing to improve security, enhanced planting around the playground and an experiment with trolleys of play equipment. Individually these were often relatively minor matters but they did nevertheless have a significant impact on the life and work of the school.

Stoll and Fink (1996: 43) offer a useful summary of school improvement that they define as a series of concurrent and recurring processes in which a school:

- enhances pupil outcomes;
- focuses on teaching and learning;
- builds the capacity to take charge of change;
- defines its own direction;
- assesses its current culture and works to develop positive cultural norms;
- has strategies to achieve its goals;
- addresses the internal conditions that enhance change;
- maintains the momentum during periods of turbulence;
- monitors and evaluates its process, progress, achievement and development.

We shall see later how governing bodies can make a significant contribution in a number of these areas.

Improving governing bodies

As we have seen, just as some schools are more effective than others, so governing bodies vary in their effectiveness. Effective governing bodies are also efficient, i.e. they are organised in such a way as to enable the governors to devote adequate time to the major educational issues in their schools. As a result of a pilot study into the role of governors in school improvement, Creese and Bradley (1997) suggested that some form of catalyst, such as a new chair of governors, an OFSTED inspection or a training event, is often required to change the way in which a governing body works. All of the research evidence (e.g. Baginsky *et al.* 1991; Creese 1993; Earley 1994; Bullock and Thomas 1997) suggests that the attitude of the headteacher is a crucial factor in determining governing body effectiveness. It may well be that headteachers and potential headteachers need further assistance to appreciate the value that an effective governing body could add to their school. That governing bodies can be of benefit to their schools rather than being a burden is a central theme of this book.

The management of change

Not all change is for the better but improvement must imply change. Change is inevitable in any organisation, being initiated from a variety of sources both from within and outside; personnel come and go and circumstances, internally and externally, change. The past fifteen years have seen tremendous changes in the educational system in the United Kingdom including the introduction of the National Curriculum and the devolution of budgetary control to individual schools through LMS. Some people resist change because it can be very unsettling, requiring a change of attitudes based upon a re-examination of basic values and beliefs, but change can be positive and invigorating, being associated with ideas of innovation, development, progression, renewal and reform (Dean 1985).

The complexity of change should not be underestimated and those responsible for planning change should always consider what it means for those who will have to implement it. For managers the key to successful change lies in helping others to understand what change really means. Change in schools may involve the introduction of new teaching material – a new curriculum; it may involve new ways of teaching – that is, different ways of presenting the material; and it may require teachers to change their fundamental ideas about the processes of learning and teaching. Typically, a major change will require change in all of these; indeed Fullan (1991) argues that there must be changes in all three of these dimensions if the innovation is to have any chance of success. He identifies three stages in the process of change: *initiation* – the sometimes lengthy process that precedes the decision to introduce the innovation; *implementation* – the introduction and initial use of the new material/ideas, which may last for two or three years; and finally *institutionalisation* – the new ways of working become embedded in the system and are no longer seen as 'new'. However, as Fullan is the first to admit, the process is not necessarily as simple or straightforward as this division into three phases suggests. Change does not proceed smoothly in a straight line; discoveries made during the implementation phase may lead to considerable modification to the decisions made in the initiation stage so that there is movement back and forth between the two phases.

Changes are often initiated by one person, or perhaps by a small group of people, and there has to be some impetus and pressure in order to introduce them because there will be many arguments for leaving things as they are. Those who initiate change have to maintain both their pressure for change and their support for those involved in the process until the new way of working has become embedded in the school's culture. However, if it is to be successful, the change must be 'owned', at least partly, by all of those involved and this implies that the originator(s) must be prepared to share their power and allow others to take responsibility.

According to Koontz and O'Donnell (1968) change is most likely to be acceptable to those concerned when:

- the nature of the proposed change is clearly understood;
- it does not threaten the security of those involved;
- those affected have helped to create it;
- it results from an application of agreed principles rather than individual diktat;
- it follows a series of successful changes;
- it starts after a previous change has been assimilated;
- it is properly planned;
- people will share in the benefits of the change;
- an organisation has been trained to accept change.

Governors and senior staff involved in the management of change should first ask themselves whether or not the proposed change is sound and if it is likely to succeed; that is, whether or not it stands a reasonable chance of eventually becoming absorbed into the school or departmental routine and culture (Everard and Morris 1996). Perfectly good innovations will not succeed if the preconditions are not right. It may be preferable to start with a relatively small-scale innovation that has a good chance of success. Further change can then be built upon the lessons learnt and the goodwill generated. Those managing the change need to be clear about the nature of the desired outcomes and to be convinced that these will be considerably better than the result of doing nothing and continuing with the status quo. They need a clear and accurate picture of the current situation, together with a clear vision of the desired end-point, and should also consider what will have been learned by themselves and their colleagues as a result of a successful innovation.

Above all, the governors and senior staff must consider the feelings of their colleagues and how to gain the commitment of at least enough of them to ensure the success of the change. There may well be certain key people within the organisation who are seen as having some influence over their colleagues. It will be helpful if the commitment of these individuals can be obtained early in the process. It may not be essential to obtain the commitment of every individual – it may only be necessary to obtain the approval of sufficient members of the organisation – the critical mass – before proceeding to implementation. Those managing change must therefore assess the present level of commitment to change and, in planning for change, include time for obtaining the required commitment through discussion and explanation, helping those involved to understand the nature of change. There must be a full recognition of the apprehension of those involved in the change and these concerns should be met as far as possible. Change cannot be avoided and therefore everything possible must be done to ensure that the process of change is a successful and positive experience for those involved. This presents a major challenge to governors and headteachers and to senior school staff as they have to manage a growing number of externally initiated changes.

The role of the governing body in school improvement

There is a clear expectation in documents emanating from Government sources that governing bodies will be involved in school improvement issues. *School Governors: A Guide to the Law* sets out the powers and duties of governing bodies, the first of which is 'deciding (with the head and the LEA if appropriate) the aims and policies of the school, and *how the standards of education can be improved*' (DfEE 1997a: 15, our italics). The broadsheet, *Governing Bodies and Effective Schools*, (DFE/BIS/OFSTED 1995) suggests that governing bodies have three main roles. These are: first, to provide a strategic view; second, to act as critical friend; and finally, to ensure accountability. It is recognised that governors have limited time and resources available and therefore the governing body 'should focus on where it can add most value – that is in helping *to decide the school's strategy for improvement*' (DFE/BIS/OFSTED 1995: 2, our italics).

However, there is, at present, little evidence of how governing bodies actually contribute to school improvement in practice. Earley (1994) found that governors generally had a rather restricted view of their role in school improvement, tending to concentrate instead on the part played by the teachers. As with the effectiveness literature, the school improvement material usually makes only a passing reference to governors, if indeed they are mentioned at all. In a diagrammatic representation of the 'layers of school improvement' (Hopkins *et al.* 1996) governors are on the outer edge, along with the National Curriculum, OFSTED and LMS. A survey of a sample of nearly a hundred reports of OFSTED school inspections (Creese 1997) shows few references to the role of the governing body in school improvement. Her Majesty's Chief Inspector of Schools in his annual reports (e.g. OFSTED 1998) comments on the shortcomings of governing bodies in terms of their involvement in strategic planning.

Some practical examples

In this volume we shall examine in some detail a wide range of examples showing how governors have contributed to improvement in their schools. Among the examples that we found in our research were the following:

Raising standards

- Governor involvement in monitoring exercises/target setting.

Enhancing quality

- Governors planning improvements to a school playground;
- Governors undertaking pupil-tracking exercises (including a child in a wheelchair);
- A governor assisting with music teaching in a junior school;
- Governor involvement in faculty/departmental reviews and evaluations.

Increasing efficiency

- Governors contributing ideas for energy conservation.

Achieving greater success in promoting pupils' spiritual, moral, social and cultural development

- Governors attending School Council meetings;
- A Governor's Pupil Services (Welfare) Group meeting pupils and parents.

Increasing the school's capacity to manage change

- Governors using business experience to improve the school's development-planning process.

The climate for improvement

Schools, departments and individuals all vary in their readiness and willingness to accept change. Hopkins and his colleagues of the 'Improving the Quality of Education for All' (IQEA) team have categorised four different types of school in terms of their attitudes to change (Hopkins *et al.* 1996):

The moving school

Key phrase: 'We try to keep abreast of developments and everything is under review.'
In such a school there is a healthy blend of change and stability, development

and maintenance. The school is relatively calm as it adapts successfully to a changing environment. Structures are adapted in line with the school's culture and traditions.

The stuck school

Key phrase: 'We've tried change before, but it doesn't work.'
The school may well be failing – conditions are poor and teaching is an isolated activity. A sense of mediocrity and powerlessness pervades, with low expectations. External conditions are blamed for the situation.

The wandering school

Key phrase: 'We've tried many new things, but nothing gets finished.'
These are schools that have experienced too much innovation. They have all of the appearance but little of the reality of change and staff are exhausted and fragmented. There is no clear route or settled destination, with no agreed central purpose to the school.

The promenading school

Key phrase: 'We're pretty pleased with things the way they are – there's no real reason to change.'
These are schools, often operating in rather traditional ways with stable staffs, living upon their past achievements. The school does not move fast or far and the little change that takes place is mainly for display. These are very difficult schools to change.

The IQEA team put forward five propositions regarding school improvement based upon their experience of working with schools. These are:

1   Without a clear focus upon the internal conditions of the school, improvement efforts will quickly become marginalised.
2   School improvement will not occur unless clear decisions are made about development and maintenance.
3   Successful school improvement involves adapting external change for internal purposes.
4   School improvement will remain a marginal activity unless it impacts at all levels across the school.
5   Data about the school's performance creates the energy for development.

With regard to the second IQEA proposition, as we shall see in Chapter 5, good development planning ensures that the school maintains a proper balance between maintenance and improvement. The planning process will inevitably throw up a wide range of possible fields for improvement. In selecting the priorities for action the governors and staff should be realistic about what they can achieve and, as far as possible, aim to tackle the changes in a logical and coherent sequence. They can also seek to ensure that their own priorities overlap or coincide whenever possible with external pressures for change (the third proposition). In their fourth proposition, Hopkins and colleagues suggest that change should impact on three levels of the organisation: the senior team (which includes the governors) responsible for setting policy, the departmental or subject team and the individual classroom teacher. Finally, schools that actively collect data about their own performance and reflect on the significance of that data show a momentum for change. Governors may be involved in the collection of the data (see Chapter 6) and can certainly help to ensure that time is made for reflection upon its significance.

The challenge for governors and senior staff is to ensure that their school remains in the 'moving' category and this means firstly that they must look to the school's internal condition and seek to foster the right climate. The IQEA team suggests that a number of factors underpin the school's improvement efforts and go to create a climate for improvement. These are:

- a commitment to staff (and governor!) development;
- practical efforts to involve staff, students, parents and the wider community in school policy- and decision-making;
- a management style that fosters leadership at all levels within the organisation and that focuses on people as much as on outcomes;
- effective co-ordination strategies;
- spending time upon enquiry and reflection (asking 'how is it going?');
- planning collaboratively.

Governors are invariably operating at one remove from the classroom and it is not always easy to show a causal link between the work of the governing body and pupil outcomes. However, during our research we found a number of examples of governing bodies making significant contributions to the climate for improvement. It is possible that their contribution in this way is at least as important as any direct contribution the governing body may make to its school's effectiveness.

Some practical examples

Demonstrating commitment to staff (and governor) development

- In one school the governors had encouraged ten staff to follow an MBA course;
- Mentor/induction programmes for new governors.

Practical efforts to involve staff, students and the community in school policies and decisions

- Governors attending meetings with parents (including new parents);
- Governors attending meetings of the pupils' School Council;
- Governors attending meetings of local residents' groups.

A management style that fosters leadership at all levels within the organisation and that focuses on people as much as on outcomes

- The governors' 'Vision Group' working to develop their vision for the school in the future;
- The headteacher and governors working together to develop the school's post-OFSTED action plan.

Effective co-ordination strategies

- Developing the role of the teacher-governor to link staff and governors more effectively;
- Governors' co-ordinating groups to ensure that the work of their separate committees was all towards the same end.

Spending time upon enquiry and reflection (asking 'how is it going?')

- Reviewing the effectiveness of the annual parent–governor meeting;
- Reviewing the work of the governing body over the previous year.

Planning collaboratively

- Joint governor–staff strategy-planning sessions;
- Joint governor–staff work on Development/Action Plans;
- Joint governor–staff training session on school improvement.

Conclusion

Schools and governing bodies vary in effectiveness; can one have an ineffective governing body in an effective school or vice versa? Figure 1.2 shows the possible combinations.

It would seem likely that an effective governing body would work to bring about improvement in an ineffective school. The evidence from OFSTED inspections suggests that ineffective schools often have less effective governing bodies, such schools often, but not always, being situated in areas of social

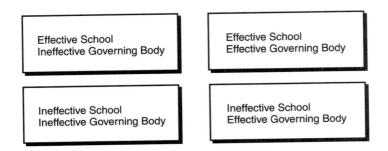

Figure 1.2 Effective schools, effective governing bodies

deprivation (Earley 1997). It is possible, of course, to have an effective school with an ineffective governing body but how much more effective might that school be with an effective governing body operating in a similar way to those reported in this book? There is a growing body of evidence that there is a significant link between an effective school and an effective governing body (Scanlon *et al.* 1999). What is not quite so clear from the research is the direction of that link.

School improvement is currently high on both the political and educational agendas. The role of governors in school improvement was first highlighted by Her Majesty's Inspectors in *Improving Schools* (OFSTED 1994b). The Government's White Paper, *Excellence in Schools* (DfEE 1997f), and the subsequent 1998 Education Act both state clearly that the purpose of governing bodies is to help to provide the best possible education for the pupils in their schools. There is a growing body of research evidence to suggest that governors, partly as a result of the inspection process, are becoming more involved in their schools and not just on the margins, but with matters related to the school's core business of teaching and learning (Earley 1998; Gann 1998). Establishing a climate for improvement is an important precondition for school improvement (Hopkins *et al.* 1996) and it appears from our research that some governing bodies are able to make a significant contribution to the establishment of this climate. Hopefully, through their involvement in target-setting and through an increased awareness of how they can contribute, governors will be enabled to assist, in a more meaningful way than hitherto, in school improvement.

We aim in this volume to provide governors with guidance, through the use of practical examples, first, of how to ensure that their governing body is efficient so that it can become effective. We then discuss the range of activities, planning, monitoring, etc., again with examples, in which governors can become involved and through which they can contribute to improvement in their schools. We would hope to see a situation in which *all* governing bodies were effective and were supporting effective schools. The research reported here is an attempt to help bring this about.

Chapter 2

The efficient and effective governing body

Introduction

For a governing body to be truly effective – to really make a difference – it has to be efficient; that is, it has to complete its tasks in the minimum of time and to the satisfaction of all concerned. Effective governing bodies are efficient in that they are able to manage their business so that the governors have time to concentrate on the key educational issues. Governors are busy people with many demands upon their time; effective time management is therefore a key issue. One way of ensuring that time is used effectively, while also making sure that important issues receive the attention they deserve, is by delegating some of the work of the governing body to committees or working parties. The key difference between the two types of group is that properly constituted committees of the governing body can have some powers delegated to them while working parties must report their recommendations back to the full governing body for action. All of the governing bodies we studied had an effective committee structure including finance committees to handle the detailed management of the school budget. Several governing bodies had set up groups specifically tasked to address what they saw as key issues for their school.

Factors contributing to an efficient and effective governing body

When governors are asked to identify what makes their governing bodies efficient and effective, the points that they list include the following:

- good teamwork and co-operation among the governors;
- an effective committee structure;
- the expertise of the headteacher and his or her attitude towards the governing body;
- a good relationship with the staff;
- a strong commitment to the school and the absence of party politics.

Other factors that governors mention include having meetings that are well chaired and managed, and having a knowledgeable clerk to the governing body.

Good teamwork

> We work closely together to secure the best that we can for the children.
>
> (Governor)

> Everyone gets on well and tries to work as a team – we are all pulling in the same direction.
>
> (Governor)

> As a governing body we all get on well together and there are excellent relationships.
>
> (Governor)

Effective teams have clear, agreed and common goals – their members must all be pulling in the same direction. Common goals may not always be self-evident in the case of a governing body, with its members chosen or elected by different interest groups, and it is therefore important that the governing body as a whole *does* discuss its purposes, aims and objectives, and reaches agreement upon them.

The role of the chair is crucial in determining the effectiveness of the team; he or she will ensure that every member of the governing body has the opportunity to contribute at meetings, summarises the discussions and makes sure that, when required, clear and definite conclusions are reached. The relationship between the head and chair is crucial; a strong sense of partnership between these two key players was noted in many of the schools. 'The combination of head and chair is the most powerful thing in a school' (Headteacher). However, the nature of the relationship must not be such that other governors feel excluded and there should be no suggestion of an 'A-team' and a 'B-team' among the governing body.

The clerk to the governing body can also play an important role in determining the effectiveness of the governing body. Some LEAs continue to offer a clerking service to their governing bodies whereby the clerk to the governing body is a member of the LEA staff. These clerks are knowledgeable, well briefed on current issues and aware of practice in other schools. They are therefore able to ensure that the governing body keeps within legal guidelines and can also offer advice on more general educational issues when required. A school secretary who takes the minutes of governing body meetings is not usually in such a fortunate position and could also be faced with conflicting loyalties between the headteacher and the governing body.

The way in which the governing body faces conflict and confronts difficult issues is an important indicator of its effectiveness. In an effective team the members support and trust one another and are able to handle conflict openly and constructively, and collective responsibility is maintained. Effective teams regularly review their operation and it should become routine that, just as the work of the school is reviewed in preparing the School Development Plan (SDP), so the governing body reviews its operations over the previous year; indeed the SDP may well include a subsection referring specifically to the governing body. Were the goals that it set itself last year achieved? If not, why not? Would changes in its working methods make it more effective? Is it necessary to consider the recruitment of new governors? What are the targets for the coming year and what training and development for governors will be required?

When a new governing body on the opening of a primary school was set up, the governors spent the first term getting to know one another and learning how to work together. This process was facilitated by a Saturday meeting of the governors at the chair's house. The day was spent working on the aims of the new school, first individually, then in pairs, fours and eights. The outcome of this exercise was then put together with the results of a similar exercise that had been carried out by the staff (teaching and non-teaching). As a result of their day together, the governors were able to set up a pattern of committees dealing with the building, finance, staffing and pupil issues; none of these was to be chaired by the chair of governors: the Curriculum Committee was deliberately constituted to consist of all members of the governing body.

Delegation and the use of subgroups

In order to manage their business more effectively, all of the governing bodies in our study had set up a number of committees. For instance, the governing body at one secondary school had a Strategic Planning Committee, Finance and General Purpose Committee, Personnel Committee, and the Pupil Services Committee (which had two subgroups dealing respectively with the curriculum and with pupil welfare). In addition there were committees to deal with health and safety issues, admissions, staff and pupil discipline and appeals. In a primary school, in addition to the governors' grievance and appeals committees, there were a finance committee and a premises working group. The curriculum group, which had never met in two years, was disbanded and the governing body as a whole dealt with curricular issues. Members of staff with responsibility for different aspects of the curriculum were invited to talk to the governing body about their work and to answer questions.

At another primary school some governors expressed concern that their meetings were dominated by papers from the LEA and that they never had the opportunity to address issues relevant to their school. The governors wanted to become more involved with how the school was going to improve and how improvement would be measured without impinging on the teachers' professionalism. In order to give governors a more positive role, three new groups were set up dealing respectively with the school environment, promotion of the school and school improvement. The remit of the finance group was widened to include offering advice and assistance on additional expenditure to these three groups.

The terms of reference of the school improvement group were to:

1   look at all of the available assessment data in the school and produce evidence of emerging trends;
2   explore ways of presenting and using additional assessment data in conjunction with that regularly produced by reading tests, SATs, etc.;
3   monitor the introduction of Baseline Assessment;
4   on the basis of conclusions reached from assessment data, make proposals for the school to consider areas for improvement;
5   contribute to the School Development Plan on the basis of perceived needs as at (4) above;
6   consider the acquisition of software or training to assist the group in the matter of interpreting statistical evidence;
7   work with the headteacher and staff to provide numerical targets for improvement.

The role of the headteacher in promoting effectiveness

> There is a sharing on the part of the head in terms of what goes on in the school.
>
> (Governor)

> The head's reports are very thorough – you get a very good and clear picture of what is going on.
>
> (Governor)

> Everyone has confidence in the head.
>
> (Governor)

Many research studies (e.g. Baginsky et al. 1991; Creese 1993; Earley 1994; Esp and Saran 1995; Shearn et al. 1995a; Scanlon et al. 1999) have identified the key role that the headteacher plays in determining the effectiveness, or otherwise, of the governing body. For instance, in one of the primary schools involved in the research, the headteacher's open style of management contributed considerably to the atmosphere of trust between her and the governors: 'The head has a very open style which involves governors' (Chair); 'I don't try to hide anything from the governors. I trust them enough to be honest with them' (Headteacher). However, both she and the chair recognise that such trust takes time to establish and has to be worked at: 'I've had to prove that what the head tells me in confidence won't go any further' (Chair). The relationship between the governors and the head is such that governors can ask questions without appearing critical: 'Questioning at meetings is done in a professional way – there's nothing personal. We don't have heated discussions because openness means that you are part way towards seeing the other point of view' (Head).

In another primary school the headteacher had encouraged governors to become fully involved in the life and work of the school ever since he was appointed. 'You can't say to governors – "we want you to be involved in this but not in that"' (Head). He believes that the ethos of the school should be a culture of improvement, involvement and evaluation – all of which are interconnected – and that this culture is founded upon the school's management structures and the governors' expectations. The governors worked with the staff on the school's aims and on the mission and vision statements. The OFSTED report on the school commented that 'there is a shared sense of purpose evident in every aspect of the school's work' and that 'There is a culture of improvement'.

Governor–teacher relationships

Governors in many of the schools were linked to individual classes or, more often in the secondary schools, to subject departments or to faculties (groups of related departments). In one of the secondary schools the governors were linked to faculties and visited regularly, which gave them a very good relationship with the staff. 'It's important that you know the staff – otherwise you're just a name' (Governor). Governors reported on their visits at meetings of the full governing body and commented on what they had seen in terms of the teaching and pupil learning and behaviour. Two of the governors had carried out pupil-tracking exercises during which they followed one child throughout the school day in order to get a 'child's eye view' of the school. Governors also worked closely with the Special Educational Needs Co-ordinator (SENCO): 'We try to let children know that we are interested in all aspects of school life' (Governor); 'We are getting away from the old-style school governor who came round once a year – governors are now very much involved with the school' (Governor). Reference is made in the next chapter to the 'adopt a governor' scheme used in a primary school, which helped to foster good relationships with the staff: 'You've got to get the confidence of teachers and pupils' (Governor); 'Staff feel that governors act in the best interests of the school – we've always felt that we were in the same boat pulling in the same direction' (Deputy Head).

The teacher-governor has an important role to play as a link between the governors and the teachers. Recent legislation means there will soon be governors elected by the members of the non-teaching or support staff to perform a similar function for them. Teacher-governors have sometimes been seen as 'second-class citizens' by some of their colleagues on the governing body and some teacher-governors have restricted their activities to acting as a watch-dog for the staff on the governing body. The best teacher-governors, while appreciating the importance of the link role, take a much broader view of their role:

It's very important to be a link between staff and governors. I use my knowledge of the curriculum to give governors something of my own to add to the governing body.

(Teacher-governor in a primary school)

Governors are almost inevitably remote from school because it is so hard for them to get involved. They rely very heavily on the head and teacher-governors to keep them informed. It's very important that teachers can bring up subjects for us to raise at the governing body – to make governors aware of staff and pupils – to represent the pupils' view.

(Teacher-governor in a secondary school)

I am a governor who can put the teachers' perspective on things. I'm not just there to put the teachers' point of view.

(Teacher-governor in a secondary school)

They recognise, however, that the role is not an easy one: 'The desire is to be a real partnership. I'm not sure that it's an achievable goal because of the gulf between staff and governors and between pupils and governors' (Teacher-governor, secondary school); 'I feel able to put forward opposing views to the heads – some heads wouldn't take kindly to that at all' (Teacher-governor, another secondary school); 'Sometimes it's difficult – I know things that I can't say to the staff' (Teacher-governor).

Governors' commitment to the school

Everyone is putting in for the good of the school and the good of the community.

(Governor)

We are all working for the good of the school – there are no ulterior motives.

(Governor)

They're there for the school and not for what they can get out of it.

(Governor)

It would seem a *sine qua non* of effective governance that all governors should demonstrate genuine commitment to their schools. This commitment would be demonstrated by regular attendance at governors' meetings (having read the appropriate papers beforehand), visiting the school regularly during the working day, attending a variety of school functions and seeking to work in a close partnership with the headteacher and staff. Experience shows that not all governors demonstrate this commitment. Some, perhaps, are not fully aware of the wide-ranging nature of their role when they become governors and find themselves unable to devote the necessary amount of time. Better briefing of prospective governors would help to avoid this. Some people seek appointment to the governing body for personal or for party political reasons and display little commitment to the education of the pupils in the schools. This is unfortunate and weakens the governing body.

Governor training

In order to be effective, all governors require a broad knowledge and understanding of their schools and of wider educational issues. In addition, some of them will probably have more specialist knowledge relating, for instance, to financial and personnel issues. Governors can gain the necessary knowledge, and have an opportunity to share ideas with governors from other schools, through the training programmes run by their LEA. A commitment to staff – and governor – training is one of the factors leading to a climate for improvement (Hopkins et al. 1996) and in all of the schools in our studies, governor training was taken very seriously. Some schools have a 'link-governor' who is responsible for liaising with the LEA Governor Training Co-ordinator and for keeping the other members of the governing body informed about the training opportunities that are available to them.

In addition to training undertaken by individual governors, many of the governing bodies in the studies had arranged training sessions of one sort or another for the whole governing body. These sessions play an important part in building the governors into an effective team. It is worth noting here the recent findings that showed a link between participation in whole governing-body training and perceptions of effectiveness (Scanlon et al. 1999). In our school-governing bodies these sessions ranged from a two-day residential weekend arranged by one of the secondary schools to a two-hour evening session with the staff in a primary school. Where governors and staff work together there are considerable benefits for the partnership between them. The off-site weekend undertaken by the governors and senior and middle managers of the secondary school was seen as having helped considerably in building the partnership: 'It pulled down some of the barriers' (Deputy head); 'It was excellent from the social point of view – it made us all feel that we were concerned about the same things' (Teacher-governor).

In another case, the headteacher of one primary school was planning a developmental meeting for staff prior to starting work on the school's development plan. At the suggestion of a member of staff, governors were invited to this session, which was held in the evening to enable governors to attend. The governors and staff were split into groups typically consisting of one teacher and two governors, and invited to undertake three exercises about the culture of the school and the school's capacity to manage change.

The induction of new governors into the team is an important aspect of governor training and development. Several of the schools in the study already had, or were planning, such schemes. In one secondary school, the governors found that some people lacked the confidence either to put themselves forward in the first place or, once appointed, found it difficult to contribute fully to the work of the governing body: 'Some governors find it difficult to contribute in meetings – they feel out of their depth. They see many of the issues discussed in governors' meetings as a long way from the children' (Chair of governors). An induction programme for new governors was set up at the instigation of one of the teacher-governors. It was hoped that this 'will not only give confidence to newly appointed governors but also lead to better retention rates and attendance at meetings' (School governing body leaflet: *An Induction for New Governors*). New governors are allocated a mentor who arranges a visit to the school for newly appointed governors, ensures that they have all of the necessary information (including a list of commonly used educational acronyms) and sits beside them during the first few governors' meetings. The system appears to be successful: 'The mentor-governor made me feel at home' (Newly appointed governor). The governors were also planning to establish a resource base for governors with appropriate documentation and similar collections of books and pamphlets were already in existence in a number of schools.

Four recently appointed governors in a secondary school produced the following list of contents for an induction programme:

- the responsibilities of governors;
- the structure of education in the area;
- meeting procedures, perhaps with a video of a governing body in action;
- an explanation of some of the educational 'jargon';
- a visit to the school (preferably a full day but certainly a half-day);
- documentation such as the school's prospectus and Development Plan;
- information about how the school is organised – 'what makes it tick';
- a list of the governors' committees and their membership and terms of reference.

Conclusion

Effective governing bodies – those that make a difference to their schools – have also to be efficient. The governors work together well and the business of the governing body is managed so that all the important issues receive proper attention. Delegating the detailed work to subgroups of the governing body is one way of improving efficiency, saving time in meetings of the full governing body while at the same time providing an opportunity for governors to pursue their own interests and to use their own expertise to the full. There should be a recognised system of reporting back so that all governors are kept informed about important decisions and there is no suspicion of A- and B-teams. The chair of the governing body and the chairs of the subgroups have an important role to play in keeping everyone 'on task', ensuring that everyone has the opportunity to contribute without allowing digressions. Governors have a responsibility to discipline themselves so that issues are not endlessly revisited, party political points are not made and hobby horses not ridden! Efficiency and effectiveness are enhanced when proper attention is paid to appropriate training for governors both individually and as a team.

The headteacher's contribution to the effectiveness and efficiency of the governing body is crucial. His or her attitude towards the governing body will be a key factor in determining the impact that the governors can have. Confident and experienced headteachers are well aware of the value of the support and involvement of their governors. These headteachers work with their staff to form a partnership with the governors based upon mutual trust and respect. In an atmosphere of openness, governors are able to contribute more fully to improvement within the school.

Effectiveness and efficiency: questions for consideration

These require clear thinking and honest answers!

1   How effective is our governing body – are we really making a difference?
2   Is the way in which our governing body operates allowing us to focus on making our school more effective?
3   Is our governing body working as an effective team?
4   Do we have an effective system of delegation?
5   How does our headteacher fully facilitate and encourage the work of the governing body?
6   Do we have a sense of partnership between the governors and the staff?
7   Do we pay enough attention to the training and development of the governors individually and collectively?
8   Are we developing as a governing body? What do we need to do to improve?

Chapter 3

The governing body, the curriculum and teaching and learning

Introduction

Teaching and learning – particularly the latter – are the central functions of any educational institution – the reason or rationale for its existence. The curriculum is the programme of learning opportunities provided by a school or college including the formal lessons in classroom, laboratory, gymnasium or on the sports field and also those activities that take place outside the normal school hours, such as dramatic and musical productions, matches against teams from other schools and school trips and visits. There is also what is termed the 'hidden curriculum' – the set of attitudes and values that the pupils or students acquire, often subconsciously, through being members of the institution. This hidden curriculum is linked closely to the ethos of the school and the relationships between pupils or students and between students and staff – and the governors. It can have a significant impact upon pupils' social and moral development.

Governors do not find their involvement in curricular matters easy: 'We have to ratify and be involved in curriculum policy and yet it would seem totally out of place for governors to be involved in the delivery of the curriculum. Therefore one doesn't actually know whether it's working' (Primary-school governor). So, in the past, many school governors have been reluctant to become too involved in the 'secret garden' of the curriculum. They have, in Joan Sallis's delightful phrase, 'been happier looking into lavatories than looking into learning'. Teachers, too, whose professional expertise is centred upon curriculum theory and pedagogical practice, have not always welcomed what they have seen as the intrusion of lay people into their expert domain. However, governing bodies have very clear curricular responsibilities and recent legislation has given governors an even greater involvement in this field whether as individuals with responsibility, say, for literacy or special educational needs or as a governing body through their involvement in setting targets for academic achievement. In this chapter we shall look firstly at governors' legal responsibilities *vis-à-vis* the curriculum and then at examples of how governors in different schools have sought to involve themselves in curricular matters – the school's core business.

Governors' responsibilities relating to the curriculum

The 1988 Education Act introduced, for the first time in this country, a National Curriculum for all pupils (with very few exceptions) in state schools between the ages of five and sixteen. Governing bodies, together with the head, are responsible for ensuring that the National Curriculum is delivered to all pupils and that its associated assessment procedures are carried out. The governors may change the LEA's curriculum policy to one that is more in line with the aims for their school, provided that the National Curriculum requirements are still met. Governing bodies in primary schools must decide whether or not the children are to receive sex education and, if they do, what form it should take; in secondary schools the governing body must have a policy on the content and organisation of the sex education programme. The governing body must also decide upon the school's approach to religious education and in controlled schools decide, after consultation with the head, upon the arrangements for collective worship.

Governors visiting their school

Governors will of course visit the school for meetings but many of these take place out of school time and the opportunity to see the school at work and the curriculum in action may be limited. However, even on these occasions, governors can view the work displayed in classrooms and, if the governors' meeting is held in a different classroom each time, the governors will be given an opportunity to see a greater variety of work. The teacher responsible for the room might be invited to say a few words about the work on show to the governors before their meeting starts. Governors will also wish to attend school functions such as plays and concerts but they should make every effort to visit their school when it is in session in order to see the curriculum in operation. These visits are made so that governors can learn about what is happening in their schools and to foster the sense of partnership between governors and staff. The frequency of such visits will depend on the individual governor's circumstances – it is more difficult for some governors to visit than others – but as an ideal every governor might aim to visit once a term. In some schools, particularly primary schools, governors may be linked to particular classes or alternatively, especially in secondary schools, they may be linked to a particular subject or curriculum area. This provides an opportunity for governors to pursue their own interests and to get to know at least some of the teachers better and to establish a good working relationship with them. Governors may find it useful to follow one particular pupil, for all or part of a day, in order to obtain a 'pupil's eye' view of the school. In one secondary school a governor spent a day with a pupil who was confined to a wheelchair in order to gain a view on how 'welcoming' the school was to disabled children and how easy it was for them to gain access to the facilities.

Vignette 3.1   Governors' visits in three primary schools

In one primary school the governors have involved themselves in an 'adopt-a-class scheme' whereby each member of the governing body is linked to a specific class and its teacher. Some of the governors are able to visit frequently, working alongside the teachers, hearing children read, working with small groups, etc. and governors with specific expertise/experience have contributed directly to the curriculum. Their support is appreciated by the teachers and has helped to develop closer relationships between governors and staff: 'It gives governors an everyday view of the realities of working in school' (Deputy head).

In another primary school the headteacher has provided guidelines for governors' visits. These helped to allay any unease on the part of the teachers and, by giving a focus to the visit, made them more productive for governors and staff. The guidelines suggest that governors should start by looking at the School Development Plan in order to identify a specific area or focus for the visit, e.g. the provision of books, positive behaviour policy, special needs, etc. The governor should then arrange an appropriate time for the visit with the head and read through any relevant papers, e.g. the school's behaviour policy. The governor should then decide specifically what he or she will look for. Examples are provided in the guidelines, which for pupil behaviour include such things as general atmosphere, how staff react to visitors, how children speak to staff and what the children have to say about the school rules. Finally, the governor is invited to consider how he or she will report on what has been observed, e.g. in a discussion with the head, an oral report to the governors or a paragraph for the annual report to parents.

In a third primary school each governor visits the school 'formally' at least once a year to see the school at work. The head and chair believe that during these visits the governors have an opportunity to match their own impressions with the information that they are given by the head: 'Governors can see that there is a calm working environment in which the children are happy' (Head). The visit begins with a briefing from the head who then shows the governor around the school, indicating any particular points of interest. The governor is then left to visit classes as he or she wishes before returning to the head for a debriefing. One governor, for instance, who teaches one day a week in another school, took a particular interest in pupils' behaviour and their listening skills. During her 'governor's visit' she went into every classroom and spent a considerable amount of time talking to the children and she also spoke to each teacher. She intended to give feedback from the results of her observations to the group of staff and governors who were revising the school's behaviour policy.

Vignette 3.2 The governors' Curriculum Committee in three schools

In our experience, almost all governing bodies have set up a Finance Committee to deal with the detail work on planning and monitoring the school's budget. Curriculum Committees were less common but are now found more frequently, especially in those governing bodies that are particularly effective. The centrality of the Curriculum Committee is stressed in one primary school by the fact that it consists of every member of the governing body. It has a very wide remit as shown by its terms of reference, which are as follows:

1   To consider and recommend to the governing body a curriculum policy for the school in line with the National Curriculum requirements and LEA guidelines.
2   To monitor implementation of the curriculum policy.
3   To participate in the development of school policies for specific curriculum areas.
4   To review the School Development Plan annually.
5   To consider and recommend to the governing body a strategy for school improvement.
6   To monitor the school's success in achieving its targets.
7   To consider the cost implications of the curriculum and to review the annual budget in line with the Development Plan.
8   To review the school prospectus.
9   To give advice to the headteacher on any matter relating to the curriculum including the assessment of pupil attainment.

In this school, every governor is linked to a curriculum area and with the appropriate member of staff (who is termed their mentor). Governors who are parents of a child in the school are deliberately not paired with their child's teacher. The mentoring process is valued by governors: 'It's good to get that little bit closer to what's going on.' After visiting the school to focus on their curriculum area, governors produce a written report for the Curriculum Committee on what they have seen and learned. These reports are kept in the folder that each governor has and help to build up a picture of the curriculum for the governing body. The list of topics suggested in the governors' folder for discussion between the governor and mentor is as follows:

1   Where are we now – what is happening at the moment?
2   How does this link to the school aims?
3   How does this link to the National Curriculum and the LEA policy statement?
4   How is this subject assessed?
5   Where are we trying to get to?
6   How are we going to get there – links to the School Development Plan?
7   What are the financial/staffing/building implications?

At another primary school, the governors have groups dealing with buildings, the curriculum, early years, finance, personnel and special educational needs (SEN) as well as a group dealing with the annual report to parents and subsequent meeting. In order to co-ordinate the work of the subgroups, reports from them are fed into meetings of the full governing body and the chairs of the subgroups meet with the chair of governors as a general-purpose group to look at broader issues. The curriculum group is chaired by a governor and consists of four governors and three teachers, including the deputy head. At a typical meeting they will hear about progress on two of the key areas identified in the school's Development Plan and review one of the school's curricular policies.

'The school's Special Needs policy includes ... the active involvement of governors' (School Prospectus). The SEN committee is chaired by the same governor who chairs the curriculum committee. She works part-time in the school teaching dyslexic children. The SEN committee discusses such matters as liaison amongst the teaching staff and between the staff and outside agencies, the implications for SEN in the school of the Government's summary of the Green Paper, *Excellence for All Children* (DfEE 1997g), and the role of the Special Educational Needs Co-ordinator (SENCO). It should be noted that at this school the concept of special needs is extended to the most able as well as to the least able: 'The governors were adamant that Special Needs should include the brightest children as well as the least able' (Governor).

The governors of a secondary school have set up a Pupil Services Committee that is divided into two halves. The curriculum group, which is chaired by the vice-chair of the governors, covers a very wide range of topics relating to curriculum issues in the school. Appropriate members of staff make presentations to the group on the curriculum areas for which they are responsible. Over the past two years the topics discussed by the group have included assessment, banding, GNVQ provision, literacy and SEN, in addition to a number of particular subject areas. The discussions are wide-ranging and can touch on subjects as diverse as the problem of litter in the school and the operation of the PTA: 'She [a named governor] keeps us on our toes, pointing out potential weaknesses' (Deputy head). At a meeting of the governors' Curriculum Committee held soon after the OFSTED inspection, the deputy head reported that the inspectors had been pleased by the way in which the group operated.

Vignette 3.3 Governors' involvement in the development of curriculum policy

Schools have policy statements or programmes, which should have been reviewed by the governors, for the various areas of the curriculum setting out what is to be taught, how and when. Conflict arose in one primary school when the governors wished to make radical changes to policy documents in which the staff had already invested a good deal of time and effort. A new system was adopted in order to reduce friction while at the same time still allowing the governors to have a meaningful input. The process now starts with a presentation on the subject by the subject co-ordinator to the full governing body at one of their termly 'special focus' meetings. The aim of the presentation is to make the governors aware of the general background before the policy is drafted or revised. Usually a governor is linked to the subject area under discussion and he or she will be involved in the detailed drafting and consultation with other members of staff that then follows. In order to ensure consistency, the governors have produced a framework for the writing of policy documents. This lists the points to be covered such as aims and objectives, the teaching and learning strategies which will be used, the arrangements for monitoring, assessment and recording, etc. The draft policy then goes for final scrutiny to the editing group, which consists of the subject co-ordinator, the governor concerned and the two deputy heads. The work of the policy-writing group plays an important part in the process of accountability within the school: 'There has to be a point at which teachers are asked to make an account without losing sight of the fact that they are professionals doing a good job of work' (Governor).

Governors' involvement in the recruitment and retention of staff

Effective learning depends upon effective teaching, delivered by enthusiastic, motivated, well-qualified and committed teachers. Governors can play an important part in the recruitment and retention of the staff – teaching and non-teaching. The school, i.e. the governing body and headteacher, should be a good employer concerned to ensure that there is a proper staff development and training programme, usually linked to the staff appraisal system and including adequate arrangements for the induction of new staff.

We have already seen in Chapter 2 that a good working relationship between staff and governors is a *sine qua non* for an effective governing body: 'You can't be a governor in a vacuum – you need to get to know the school, to be part of the place. To be an effective governor you have to be part of the life of the school' (Governor); 'You can loiter with intent in the staff room' (Governor); 'It's important that you know the staff – otherwise you're just a name' (Governor).

The close involvement of governors in their schools contributes to a very good relationship between staff and governors. For instance, one chair of governors tries to visit every classroom once or twice a term and to talk individually to every member of staff, and she also has coffee in the staff room at break. In this school, as in many others, there is a strong partnership between the head and chair: 'There mustn't be anything to hide between staff and governors' (Chair); 'I share everything with the chair. That trust takes time to build' (Head).

However, a school's success depends upon the contribution of *all* of its staff; a point which will be emphasised by the appointment of a representative of the non-teaching or support staff to the governing body. Some schools are using the Investors in People Standard as a way of demonstrating their commitment to the development and training needs of their staff. The fundamental purpose of the Standard is 'to raise the performance of an organisation through the effective development of all staff' (DfEE 1997b). This programme promotes a whole-school approach, which includes the governors, to developing the skills of the staff, linking individual training and development with the targets set by the school.

Vignette 3.4   Governors and the appointment of staff

Governors have their most direct impact upon teaching and learning when they appoint a new member of staff and the more senior the appointment, the greater the impact is likely to be. It follows, therefore, that governors should be prepared to devote time and effort to the whole selection process from identifying the vacancy, to making the appointment and debriefing the unsuccessful candidates. Except in the case of the appointment of the headteacher – the most crucial decision for good or ill that a governing body can make – the governors will be working very closely with the headteacher. In one primary school the governors and headteacher, with the assistance of the LEA link primary adviser, wrote a detailed 'person specification' in addition to the job description when appointing a new deputy head. The four candidates to be interviewed were chosen by a small group consisting of the chair of governors, another governor, the head and the LEA adviser. The candidates all visited the school before the day of the interviews and the headteacher went to see them at work in their classrooms in their own schools. This practice is unusual and may be prohibitively expensive. An alternative may be to invite each of the candidates, forewarned of course, to work with a small group of children for a short period at the school on the day of the interviews, observed by some or all of the members of the selection panel.

The selection process began with the four candidates making individual presentations to the four governors and headteacher on the topic of 'the challenge of the able child'. The governors were provided with copies of a pro forma on which to record their impressions of the candidates. The style and content of the presentations were to form a significant part of the appraisal of the candidates and were frequently referred to as the selection panel made their choice. This was the first time that presentations had been used in this way as part of the selection process at the school and the governors found them very valuable: 'The presentations raised a number of areas to pursue in the interviews' (Governor); 'The presentations gave an idea of what the candidates saw as important' (Governor).

After a break for coffee, the candidates and governors together toured the school. At this stage the governors were keen to see how far the candidates were prepared to engage with the pupils and other members of staff. A buffet lunch was arranged for the candidates to which all the staff and governors had been invited to give them an opportunity to meet the candidates. In the afternoon the final interviews took place after which there was a very perceptive and thorough discussion of the strengths and weaknesses of the four candidates and, at the end of their deliberations, the selection panel unanimously agreed to recommend the appointment of one of the candidates (who accepted the post) to the full governing body.

Selection is to some extent a two-way process; while the governors hope to select the best possible candidate for the post, the candidates themselves will be weighing up the school. The way in which the selection process is arranged and the manner in which they are treated will contribute to their view of the school – to deciding whether or not this is a school in which they would wish to work. The school will not wish high-quality candidates to withdraw from the interview process.

Issues arising from the vignettes

Governors can learn about the curriculum in a variety of ways: by reading appropriate documents, by receiving reports from the headteacher or through presentations by different members of staff about their work. However, valuable though these all are, they are no substitute for the direct knowledge and awareness that the governor acquires through seeing the curriculum in action in the classroom. The first vignette illustrates the value of these visits to both staff and governors. Only by actually visiting the school and seeing it at work will governors learn what it is really like. Governors who may have had no contact with education since they themselves were at school need to remember that things have changed in education in the last twenty or thirty years, as in all aspects of life. Governors are sometimes uncertain about how to behave and staff can be uneasy if they are uncertain of the governors' role and expectations. In such circumstances, some agreed guidelines can be immensely helpful to both sides. Governors must always remember that they are *not* inspectors and that they are visiting as friends and supporters of the school. They are there in order to gain knowledge and information about the school and about education in general, and to become more fully integrated into the school team. Governors' visits to the school offer an excellent opportunity to monitor progress; the list of topics for discussion between governor and teacher-mentor given in Vignette 3.2 provides an excellent starting point for this process. We shall discuss governors' role in monitoring more fully in Chapter 6.

A Curriculum Committee provides an opportunity for the exploration of curricular issues in greater depth than may be possible in a normal meeting of the full governing body. Whether or not such a group consists of all or some of the governors is a matter for decision but, given the centrality of the curriculum, there should be some mechanism through which some, at least, of the governors are closely involved in these issues. Curricular policies are an obvious example of something that could be on the agenda of such a group though governing bodies in different schools will choose to handle policy-making in differing ways; indeed a governing body may choose not to handle apparently similar issues in the same way. Linking individual governors to classes or to subject areas is another very useful way of bringing governors into regular contact with the school's curriculum and teaching and learning. Governors need to be assisted by the staff to overcome their, perhaps natural, diffidence; governors need to be helped to ask the right questions.

Above all, because this is where they can have the most direct impact on what is happening in the classrooms, governors must do all that they can in order to ensure that the school attracts, selects and retains good teachers. The more senior the appointment, the more important it is that the selection process is so arranged as to ensure that the best possible candidate, who fully meets the school's needs, is selected.

Governors may have experience of staff selection in other fields and, in any case, they offer a different perspective from the professional educators. A governor can look at a candidate and think 'Would I be happy for this person to be teaching my child? What sort of personal qualities and characteristics will she or he bring to the school?' Once a member of staff has been appointed the governors should ensure that the school is seen as a 'good employer' with, for instance, proper arrangements for on-going staff development including an induction programme for all new members of staff (and governors). If there is high morale and motivation among the staff then the teachers are much more likely to deliver a quality experience for the pupils. A school is only likely to be as good as its most important – and, of course, most expensive! – resource, its people.

Conclusion

In all of the schools in our study, governors were involved in the discussion of curricular issues. Creese and Bradley (1997) noted in their pilot study that governors appeared more likely to take an active part in curricular discussions if they felt that they had a basis of knowledge from which to start. Thus, in one school, the governors in a working party dealing with pupil behaviour felt more confident and able to contribute than they did when working on the school's sex education policy. In the first case they felt that they had first-hand experience of children's behaviour, while the expertise was thought to reside solely with the staff on matters of sex education. Governors should do all that they can to familiarise themselves with curricular issues, particularly by visiting the school when it is in session. The professionals, including governor trainers, have a role to play in assisting governors to gain the knowledge base from which they can comfortably engage in discussion of the curriculum issues.

Governors and the curriculum: questions for consideration

1   How knowledgeable are governors about the school's curriculum? How knowledgeable do they need to be?
2   Are the appropriate curricular policies in place?
3   Do governors visit classrooms regularly?
4   Would there be benefits in linking governors to classes/subject areas?
5   Is there a governors' Curriculum Committee? Is it effective?
6   Are governors effectively involved in the development of curricular policies?
7   Is the school's process for the appointment of staff sufficiently developed so as to ensure that the best candidates for the school are selected?
8   Is the school a good employer? Are there adequate arrangements for staff training and development including an induction programme?

Chapter 4

The role of the governing body in strategic planning

Introduction

> We need to be better at targeting the really big issues and giving ourselves time to discuss them. We need to be better in terms of the process; in the way in which we tackle issues.
>
> (Governor)

> The key is prioritising – only tackling those things we think are important.
>
> (Governor)

These comments, from governors in two different schools, reinforce a point made in the broadsheet, *Governing Bodies and Effective Schools* (DFE/BIS/OFSTED 1995), which defines the provision of a strategic overview as the first of a governing body's three main roles. As the pamphlet points out, a governing body has important duties and responsibilities but that there is a limit on the amount of time that governors can place at the disposal of their schools. Talking to governors, all too often one hears anecdotes of governors' meetings that are over-long and dominated by trivial matters. It is all too easy for governors to become too closely involved in the minutiae of matters concerning finance and the premises – matters with which they feel familiar and comfortable – and to neglect the more important educational issues. It is important that governors should use their limited time to best effect and the broadsheet suggests that one key area in which governors should be involved is in helping to plan the school's strategy for improvement. In their reports, OFSTED inspectors comment on the lack of involvement by some governing bodies in strategic planning and commend those governing bodies who are involved in this way.

Governing bodies need to develop a balance in their work between 'maintenance' activities that are essential to keeping the school running smoothly and 'developmental' work that seeks to provide for future improvement. The way in which a governing body manages its business is important in allowing governors time to address the long-term issues and preventing them from becoming bogged down in matters of routine. The headteacher is responsible for the day-to-day management of the school and governing bodies will normally not be involved in such matters. Another way by which governors can ensure that time is available for the big issues is to delegate detailed work to standing committees or to *ad hoc* working groups.

What is strategic planning?

Every school should have a Development or Improvement Plan that sets out, in some detail, its priorities for development during the school year. This plan will normally indicate precisely who is responsible for each of the items listed and include time-scales, details of targets to be achieved and the resources allocated. This plan will almost certainly be linked to the action plan that was written as a result of the most recent inspection of the school by OFSTED inspectors. By contrast, strategic planning is concerned with the medium- and long-term future of the school – anything from, say, two to five years ahead. There is a certain element of crystal-ball gazing in the process as governors and staff try to assess what the school might reasonably be expected to have achieved in this period. The plan should have a coherence and a structure, rather than being a series of disconnected and random ideas, and the impact of outside influences must be considered where possible. These might include, for instance, matters such as changes in government and/or LEA policy or changes in demography within the school's locality. Strategic planning also has to be realistic in terms of the resources that are likely to be available; it would be pointless to plan for, say, an increase in staff when pupil numbers appear likely to decline. Governors working in this way and who have developed a long-term vision that is shared by staff and parents will be in a better position to control events rather than being totally at the mercy of outside influences. The process is not easy: governors have to be confident, able to detach themselves from immediate concerns and aware of the range of options open to them.

Vignette 4.1   The governors' Vision Group in a primary school

Following a suggestion in their OFSTED report, the governors of a primary school set up a small group to consider their long-term vision for the school. At their first meeting the group, which consisted of the head, chair and two other governors, drew up a 'spider diagram' that posed a series of questions about the future direction of the school (see Figure 4.1).

This diagram (which is reproduced, as is Figure 4.2, by kind permission of the governors and headteacher of the school) was then presented to a meeting of the full governing body. Although it was felt to be a good beginning, there was uncertainty about how best to move forward: 'There must be a process, a sequence, to reach a strategic plan. It's about identifying the process' (Governor).

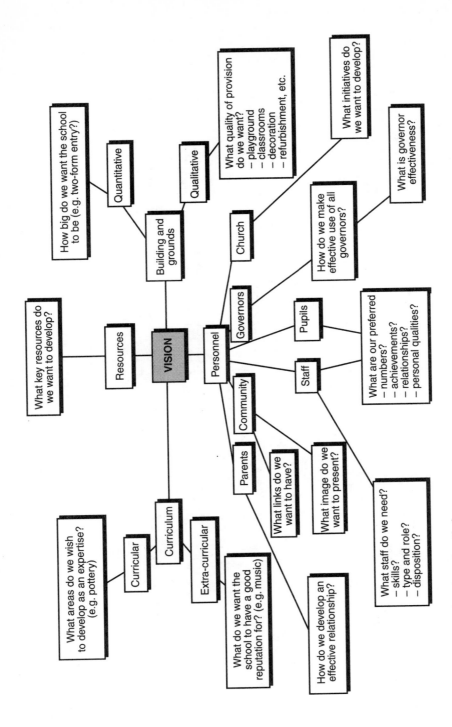

Figure 4.1 A vision for the school's future

Aim	Questions	Outcome
1. Improved understanding of roles and stronger fulfilment of responsibilities	Of the governors' responsibilities: • Know the school • Link the school to the community • Advise and support • Plan for the future and improvement • Promote the school • Ensure an effective team • Monitor the work of the school 1. How do governors do these effectively? (What do governors actually do?)	A stronger sense of purpose (measured by survey?) Increased involvement of individual governors
2. To change and grow as a governing body	2. Where are we now – do we have a common view? 3. Where would we like to be? 4. Where do we have to be?	Ability to meet change in a controlled fashion
3. To improve effective participation and teamwork	5. Do we use time and talents effectively/efficiently? 6. Do governors feel valued, equal members of a team?	A common sense of purpose and greater satisfaction
4. To communicate effectively	7. Do governors communicate effectively? • Build relationships with stakeholders? • Do teachers know (like) what governors do? • Do parents?	Improvement in (measured) perception of governors' role

Figure 4.2 Suggested aims/outcomes for the personnel (governors) theme

Following this meeting of the full governing body, the Vision Group met again to consider how to proceed. One of the governors suggested that there were four key themes in the spider diagram: building and grounds, curriculum, resources and personnel. (The last theme was later subdivided into six sections covering staff, pupils, parents, governors, church and community.) Specific aims could be developed for each of these themes, which could then be prioritised with consideration being given to the ease with which they could be achieved and the resources needed to achieve each of them. Once priorities had been agreed, detailed action plans could then be developed. It was agreed that prioritisation would be the key and most difficult task and that there would need to be consultation with other governors, the staff, parents and the wider community (including the LEA).

During this and at two subsequent meetings of the group, each of which lasted for about two hours, the four key areas were considered in turn in detail with a range of questions being listed for each. The questions were written up on a white-board so that all could see them easily and contribute to the discussion. (With the benefit of hindsight, it might have been preferable to use a flip-chart so that the pages could be taken away and written up subsequently rather than having to have a copy made from the board at the time.) The governor who had suggested this approach wrote up the outcomes of the meetings so that they were available for distribution to all governors. He grouped the questions that had emerged into aims that were subdivisions of the overall themes and included the hoped-for outcomes for each aim. Figure 4.2 shows an example of one of the completed sheets.

At their fifth meeting the Vision Group worked on these aims, attempting to prioritise them. At the suggestion of the governor who had prepared the sheets, they rated each of the aims for importance/urgency on a score of one to ten, with those aims that were perceived by the group as more important receiving the higher score. The aims were also rated for 'do-ability', i.e. cost/time needed/complexity on a scale of one to five. Scoring in this way gave greater weight to importance and urgency than to do-ability; the maximum possible score would be fifteen for an aim that was seen as extremely important and urgent, and yet easy to accomplish.

In prioritising their aims the governors recognised that it might not always be necessary to attend to an aim as a matter of urgency but that it might be important to begin to assemble some data on the present situation with regard to that point: 'Until we've measured, we don't know if we've got a problem' (Governor). The members of the group also clearly recognised the importance of sharing their ideas with others: 'They [the other governors and staff] have got to buy into it' (Governor). Accordingly, the Vision Group presented their ideas to the next meeting of the full governing body. The governors were reminded that the point of the exercise was to try to determine what would characterise their school compared to other schools in the area in five to ten years' time. The governors were then divided into three groups and given slips of paper with the top twenty or so aims that had emerged as the Vision Group's priorities in their work. The three groups, each of which contained at least one member of the Vision Group, were asked to prioritise the aims into four groups: things to tackle now, in two years' time, in five years' time, and perhaps not at all. After about half an hour the groups shared their results. It has to be said that there was a considerable amount of divergence in the views of the three groups but that, nevertheless, half a dozen of the aims did emerge as being seen by the governors as a whole as the most important.

Following this meeting, the group reconvened in order to determine how to proceed. It was decided to take as their priorities those determined jointly by the Vision Group and by the governing body as a whole. The first batch of these was to:

1   Identify and plan to improve the balance of skills among the staff. (This had been rated very highly by the Vision Group but less highly by the governing body.)
2   Identify the potential for growth in the numbers on roll, and develop plans to accommodate that growth. (The most highly rated of the governing body's priorities.)
3   Identify and strengthen those areas of the curriculum that will characterise the school.
4   Understand and improve the relevance of school–parent communication.
5   Exploit under-used space more fully.

It was agreed that these areas would now be delegated to designated individuals and groups for further more detailed work. Reports from these individuals/groups would go to the full governors' meeting and appropriate action would then be built into the Development Plan.

Vignette 4.2   Governors' involvement in strategic planning in a secondary school

> At the end of the day they [the governors] are responsible for the school and their input is crucial. They bring expertise, parental concerns and staff concerns.
>
> (Teacher-governor)

> It's vitally important that governors do input into the plan.
>
> (Governor)

A secondary school has a long-term Development Plan in addition to its annual plans, the first of which, designed to cover the period 1994–9, was very sharply focused on the school's survival (pupil numbers were very low when the plan was prepared). The plan was developed, in part at least, during a weekend session for governors that was led by a governor who was the manager of a local chemical plant: 'This was very effective due to the input of one governor' (Teacher-governor).

More recently, the headteacher, wishing to start with a more classroom-based process, invited the staff to set out their priorities for development. Governors were invited to contribute to the process at a Saturday morning session that was attended by ten governors (including both of the teacher-governors). The meeting started with the head reminding the governors of the priorities set out in the previous long-term plan. He believed that the situation had now changed (the school was now over-subscribed for instance) and that many of the original priorities had been attained. It was therefore time to have a fresh look at the long-term aims. The original planning process had been very much 'top-down' but he hoped now to be able to achieve a more 'bottom-up' model. He outlined some of his concerns for the future and shared with the governors the outcomes of the staff exercise in the course of which the teachers had identified a number of priorities for the future.

The governors were then invited to identify *their* priorities for future development. They were provided with a pro forma that asked them to consider, for each of the priorities that they had identified, where the school was now, and where, ideally, they would like it to be. The governors then split into three groups. After about half an hour the groups came together again and the following areas were identified as key concerns:

- the need to increase the school's cash input per capita;
- the need to develop pupils' motivation and sense of social responsibility;
- the need to develop further links with the local community and to provide activities for young people outside of normal school hours;
- the need to enhance the staff support system;
- greater integration of the governing body with the staff;
- the need to improve the school's public image.

It was a very thoughtful session with the governors recognising that these priorities were, to a large extent, interrelated; the governors were concerned as much, if not more, about the quality of life that pupils would experience in the future as they were about academic results. Four of these priorities (cash input, governing body integration, the place of the school in the community and developing students' social responsibility) had not emerged during the staff's discussions.

After the plenary feedback, there was a break for coffee before the governors divided into three groups again: 'I want us to get beyond just identifying priorities and to try to move into strategic planning. I want some concrete ideas as to how we might achieve our ideal' (Head). Governors were provided with a pro forma entitled 'Our high school – medium-term planning'. There were four columns headed: 'Where are we now?'; 'What would the area look like in a perfect school?'; 'What needs to be done?'; and 'What resources/people/things would we need?' The governors tackled two issues in their groups: the school in the community and greater integration of the governing body. After group discussion there was another plenary session during which the points that had emerged relating to these two areas were shared.

On the place of the school in the community it was felt that in a perfect school there would be many people coming into the school and many students going out into the community, for example, on work placements, community projects, etc. Community links were potentially very wide-ranging involving feeder primary schools, adult education, links with sports teams who use the school's facilities, local businesses and tenants' and residents' associations, etc. In order to support further development in this area there was a need for resources, e.g. for the arts centre, for supervision outside normal school hours and for planning and design of (for example) an adventure playground.

In the discussions of how the governing body might become more closely integrated into the school, it was recognised that there was a committed governing body with a record of achievement. However, the view was expressed that too much time was spent in meetings that tended to be rather divorced from the school. There was not enough contact between the governors and the staff and pupils. It was felt that more contact would lead to greater mutual understanding. Various suggestions were made as to how greater contact might be arranged.

The next stage was to be the further development of these ideas by the steering group. It was recognised that more time could usefully have been spent on the exercise but: 'This has been really worth doing; it's the meeting where we talk about the school' (Governor).

Issues arising from the vignettes

Both governing bodies set a significant amount of time aside specifically for their planning exercises; attempts to undertake this sort of work at the end of the agenda of a normal governors' meeting are unlikely to be very successful. The Vision Group at the primary school took nearly ten hours to reach the stage of prioritising described in the vignette. The governors in the secondary school spent three hours and needed at least twice as long if they were to address satisfactorily all the points that they had raised. Another point for a governing body to consider is how many governors will be involved: is it to be a small group, as was the case in the primary school, or open to all interested governors as it was in the secondary school? Whether all of the governors are involved or not, careful consideration needs to be given to how ideas emerging from the planning group will be shared with others involved. All of the stakeholders need to be kept informed and to have the opportunity to contribute their own ideas as the plan develops.

Both groups of governors met in their schools, one in the evenings and one on a Saturday morning. Obviously the time of meetings has to be chosen for the convenience of the governors involved but there may be something to be said for avoiding, if at all possible, too many evening meetings when everyone is tired after a day's work. Consideration might also be given to meeting away from the school in a neutral, and perhaps more comfortable, environment. Wherever and whenever the group meets, thought should be given to the provision of appropriate refreshments and to resources that will facilitate the governors' work such as flip-charts, white-boards and pro formas.

Many ideas for future development are likely to emerge during the initial stages of the planning process and it is important to have some process for prioritising these. One method has already been described; the staff and governors of another primary school used another approach. The governors and staff met initially as two separate groups and each individual was asked to write down on cards nine things that he or she would like to see happen. The governor or teacher then arranged the nine cards in the form of a diamond with their first priority at the top, then their second and third priorities, their fourth, fifth and sixth priorities on the middle row, and so on down to their last card. It was reported that the governors tended, as did the governors at the secondary school, to come up with wider and more general issues than the members of staff. After each individual had prepared his or her diamond, they paired up with a colleague to produce their joint set of priorities and the pairs then joined up to form quartets. Since the staff had met first, their finalised set of priorities could be shown to the governors as they progressed through the exercise and the headteacher pulled the staff and governor outcomes together to form the final document. A note was kept of the original diamonds so that there was an opportunity to look back to check to ensure that nothing of significance had been overlooked.

Conclusion

The vignettes illustrate how two different governing bodies tackled strategic planning in their very different situations. Probably the most significant point to emerge is the amount of time taken to prepare a strategic plan. It should be remembered, however, that this is an activity that governors and staff will only undertake every four or five years. It is also significant that both governing bodies came up with the idea of improving their own practice and relationships with staff and parents. This helps to demonstrate the governors' commitment to improvement in a very practical way. The contribution of two individual governors, at the secondary school in producing their first long-term plan and at the primary school in the events described, is also noteworthy. These governors were able to use their management experience, gained elsewhere, to help their schools to move forward.

Strategic planning: questions for consideration

Governing bodies, especially those tackling this process for the first time, might find it useful to address these questions:

1   How many governors will be involved in the planning process?
2   How will sufficient time be found?
3   Where and when will the group meet?
4   What facilities/resources will be required to facilitate the meeting(s)?
5   How will ideas be shared between the stakeholders?
6   By what system will ideas be prioritised?

Chapter 5

Target-setting and school improvement planning

Introduction

Drawing up a strategic plan for a school's development will not, by its very nature, be an annual event. Each year, however, schools draw up what are termed School Development Plans (SDPs) or, increasingly, School Improvement Plans (SIPs). The Development or Improvement Plan sets out the school's priorities for action over the next two to three years and is, or should be, the key document underpinning school improvement. The SDP/SIP helps the school to know where it is heading, which, in school effectiveness and improvement terms, is towards better learning experiences and outcomes for pupils (Stoll and Fink 1996). All other plans, including the budget and the staff development programme, should revolve around the Development or Improvement Plan. The plan might usefully include a section relating to the governors' priorities for their own development over the next twelve months or so. In addition to bringing together all aspects of the school's planning, the SDP/SIP helps the school to maintain its focus on its educational aims and turns the long-term vision of the strategic plan into short-term goals. Development planning is now firmly established as a key strategy for school improvement and schools are now incorporating targets – particularly pupil performance targets – within their plans.

Target-setting is a school improvement strategy that forms a central plank of the Government's drive to raise standards and should be an integral part of the planning process. Since September 1998 governing bodies have had a statutory responsibility to ensure that targets have been set by their schools in certain key areas and that these have been reported to parents. This chapter explores the issues surrounding the role of the governing body in target-setting and relates them to the cycle of School Self-Improvement. This cycle underpins the process and is increasingly seen as an integral part of School Development and Improvement Plans. Governors, it is suggested, as part of development planning, should support the head and staff in working through a five-stage cycle of school improvement that gives emphasis to pupil performance (DfEE 1997d).

It is for each governing body to decide how governors are to be involved in the planning process which is, or should be, an ongoing cyclical programme. Inspection evidence and research (e.g. Cuckle *et al.* 1998) has shown that governing bodies vary in the way they carry out their responsibilities. It is worth remembering, therefore, that 'where governing bodies are fully involved in their school's planning they are better informed and have more effective oversight of the conduct of the school' (OFSTED 1994b: 52). Some governing bodies are involved in the planning process from a very early stage and help to shape priorities and give direction to the school; others prefer to leave a greater degree of responsibility with the headteacher and staff. The respective roles and responsibilities of the governing body and the headteacher need to be worked out by the various parties in a way that makes sense to them. Useful advice on this is provided by the document, *Guidance on Good Governance* (DFEE 1996). Headteachers and governors should aim to develop a good working partnership, with the head providing the governing body with 'the information, advice and recommendations it needs to carry out its functions effectively and *to understand how the school is performing*' (DfEE 1996: 7, our italics).

Promoting a climate of self-evaluation and review

Governing bodies will very rarely make a *direct* impact upon the quality of teaching and learning in the school, or in raising pupils' or teachers' standards of achievement. We have, however, already drawn attention in Chapter 1 to the considerable *indirect* contribution that governors can make to the development of their schools by promoting a climate in which questions about *performance* – including their own – are openly and honestly discussed. The role of the governing body as 'critical friend' is crucial. *Critical* in the sense of the governing body's responsibility for reviewing the school's effectiveness, asking challenging questions and pressing for improvements; a *friend* because it exists to promote the interests of the school and its pupils. It is possible to create a climate for critical self-evaluation but only where there is openness, honesty and trust on the part of *all* concerned. Such relationships cannot be legislated for or introduced overnight! Considering the following questions may give governors and heads insights into the extent to which a climate for improvement exists at the school:

Does a climate for improvement exist at the school?

- Is there an acceptance that the governing body has a role in discussing matters to do with school improvement?
- Can governors raise challenging questions without being perceived as confrontational or unsupportive of the school?

- How does the head keep governors informed about the school's performance?
- Can governors discuss performance issues without being seen as intruding on the ground of the professionals?
- Do governors still feel as though they are being critical if they want to talk about improving on past performance or raising standards?
- Are there areas of the school that are highly valued but where information about performance is not collected?
- Is a balance achieved between discussing the school's performance and ensuring the governing body does not interfere in the responsibilities of the school's senior staff?

As outlined in Chapter 1, the notion that *you don't have to be ill to get better* is one that underpins much improvement work – and not only in schools. The thinking behind various 'quality initiatives' (e.g. TQM, the British Quality Foundation) that some governors may use in their own work settings may be equally valuable to schools. For the governing body to operate in this way there is a need not only for performance information (at both national and local level) but also for support and training to assist governors and headteachers to use these data to good effect. Although some schools have been using performance information in this way for some time, most governing bodies and many headteachers have, until now, had little direct experience of target-setting and may therefore require training and support.

Planning for improvement

A model that schools and governors are now being encouraged to use to underpin the planning and target-setting process is the *'five-stage cycle for school self-improvement'* (DfEE 1997c; 1997d). The aim of this cycle is to encourage schools and their governing bodies to review and improve their performance, ensuring that pupil achievement remains at the centre of all that is done. The target-setting cycle for school self-improvement is seen as the next step in improving the process of Development Planning in schools. The school's targets for improvement need to be an integral part of its planning. The self-improvement cycle is set out in Figure 5.1 and the various ways in which the governing body might be involved in each of the five stages of the cycle is discussed below.

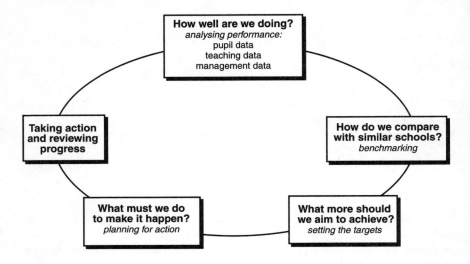

Figure 5.1 The cycle of school self-improvement

Stage 1: How well are we doing? Analysing performance

Effective development and improvement planning starts with a review or audit of the work of the school that should identify the school's current strengths and weaknesses, and be a basis for selecting the priorities for development. Only by establishing clearly the present position in the school is it possible to plan properly how to achieve improvement. The governors and senior staff need detailed, accurate and up-to-date information on which to base their decision-making. This information might include:

- pupil performance data (e.g. examination results or Key Stage assessments or attitudinal data);
- information on teaching performance (e.g. based on appraisal);
- school management data (e.g. based on inspection and self-evaluation/internal review).

It is important to include 'soft' (e.g. pupil attitudes to learning) as well as 'hard' (e.g. pupil attainment) information. In this way school governing bodies can ensure they have information about that which they *value* rather than only about that which is easy to measure – 'We must learn to measure what we value, not simply value that which can be easily measured!'

The headteacher and other senior managers of the school should, of course, be a major source of information about the school's performance in a whole range of different areas, including pupil performance. If such information is not readily available or there is a reluctance for it to be shared, governors have a right to ask for it. It is impossible for the governing body to perform its key tasks without knowing what is happening. Does the head's termly report to the governing body, for example, contain sufficient information about what's going on? Schools can enlist the help of outside agencies to assist with the audit, can use one of the many published schemes of school evaluation or review, perhaps an LEA scheme, the OFSTED handbook (OFSTED 1998a) or an approach of their own devising. The school can also make good use of comparative performance data provided by the LEA and Government agencies.

This stage in the cycle can be mismanaged through the collection of too much information; schools often collect more evidence than they find time to analyse and there is usually no shortage of data available. Governors can usefully ask what information already exists and what the school is doing with it. The time involved in undertaking a very wide-ranging review should not be under-estimated and it may be better for governors and staff to concentrate upon one small part of the work of the school at first, especially if this is an area that has already been recognised as in need of improvement or one in which there is a need to set targets. The audit may reveal unsuspected strengths, weaknesses that are easily remedied or the need for more detailed investigation.

For this first stage in the target-setting cycle it is worth remembering the 'Monitoring and Evaluating Performance' questions in the Governing Bodies and Effective Schools (DFE/BIS/OFSTED 1995) pamphlet, namely:

- How is our school currently performing?
- Are some parts of the school more effective than others and, if so, why?
- Are some groups of pupils doing better than others and, if so, why?
- How does the school's achievement now compare with previous years?
- How does the school's performance compare with that of other similar schools?

Stage 2: How do we compare with similar schools? Benchmarking

For governing bodies to support school improvement effectively, information about the performance of their own and similar schools is required. In this second stage of the improvement cycle, the school's performance is compared with those of other schools that are of a similar kind or who have many characteristics in common. This process is sometimes referred to as benchmarking and it is relatively new to education. Benchmarking is the process of measuring actual performance against the performance of others who share broadly similar characteristics.

Performance and assessment data (PANDAs), provided each autumn by OFSTED, is a very important source of information for schools and governors. Other useful performance data are 'value added analyses' of pupils' academic progress over time in schools. Benchmark data and 'value-added' measures enable schools to understand their impact on pupils' progress, to go beyond league tables and to make like-with-like comparisons between themselves and other schools. It is important to know how the school is doing relative to similar schools, and how the pupils are performing – in both academic and other areas – relative to similar pupils elsewhere. Schools and governors also need information about performance trends locally and nationally. National agencies, such as OFSTED, the Qualifications and Curriculum Authority (QCA) and most LEAs, are producing a range of performance measures that provide benchmarks to support schools and governors in setting challenging and realistic targets for improvement.

Asking questions about the school's comparative performance will ultimately help in understanding how well the school should be doing. But it is important to recognise that benchmarks are not targets – they represent the performance achieved by the *best* members of a like-minded group. Benchmarks do not tell schools what targets to set themselves. As such, benchmarks offer a challenge to schools, indicating as they do the results achieved by the best of the group given, for example, similarities of pupil intake and background factors. Governing bodies have an important role at this stage of the cycle to ensure that factors influencing current performance have been adequately discussed by the school and that fair and reasonable comparisons are being made. Has the school sought advice on these matters from LEA advisers or other consultants? If not, should such activity be approved and funded or is the school confident that its own analyses are sufficient?

Governors might not know the answers to such questions but they should at least know how to ask them. The interpretation of information is as important as its availability – 'a view from the outside' from both external consultants, inspectors or a working party of staff and governors can be most helpful in knowing *'how do we compare with similar schools?'*

Stage 3: What more should we aim to achieve?
Setting the targets

Goal, objective, purpose, aim, ambition, intention, hope, wish – these are all words that are often used to indicate where we are going or where we would like to be. Targets and target-setting are similarly about intentions and plans for the future but what marks them out from the others is that they include details of how they will be achieved. Target-setting within education is an approach to raising standards in schools by establishing goals – which are quite specific and measurable – for improved pupil performance. Target-setting puts the performance of pupils – both their academic performance and their performance in other areas valued by schools, governors and parents – at the centre of things. All governing bodies must ensure their schools set agreed targets for pupil performance that, if met, will normally lead to year-on-year improvement. By raising their own standards of achievement in this way each school is contributing to raising levels of attainment both locally – each LEA has its own targets to achieve in numeracy and literacy – and nationally.

During the *target-setting* stage the headteacher and staff, working closely with the governing body, should agree on clear, achievable, challenging and measurable targets for pupil performance as well as for improving other aspects of the school (e.g. school policies and procedures, teaching strategies). These are built into the Development or Improvement Plan and reflect the school's priorities. The targets that are set are based on an analysis of the school's current performance, and how this compares with that of similar schools, and also reflect the school's educational priorities which the governors will have helped shape. Governors can contribute to the process by asking appropriate questions and seeking advice from the professionals from within the school, the LEA and elsewhere. Whatever the targets agreed, they will need to be SMART. These are:

- Specific;
- Measurable and manageable;
- Achievable, appropriate and agreed;
- Relevant, realistic and recorded;
- Time-related.

'Outcome' targets are those that are couched in terms of *what pupils will achieve*. They are about what pupils will do as a result of the targets set. Examples of targets to be achieved over the next two years might be to:

- increase the number of Key Stage 2 pupils achieving Level 4 or better to 65 per cent;
- increase the number of pupils obtaining C or better at GCSE in a subject to 55 per cent;
- ensure all pupils at Key Stage 1 get at least Level 1 in Maths;
- increase the range of purposes pupils write for in Key Stage 2;
- increase the average point score of GCSE pupils to forty-four;
- raise the proportion of pupils leaving school who hold a positive self-image;
- raise the level of pupil involvement in extra-curricular activities by 20 per cent.

When agreeing targets it is helpful to recognise that the ability of different year groups may vary. This means that on occasions targets set may be lower than in previous years. Random fluctuations in school performance are, therefore, more likely to be identified if a longer time period is agreed. A three-to-five-year 'rolling average' gives a fairer picture of school performance. It is also worth noting that percentages are not always appropriate to use, especially when the number of pupils is low.

Targets are unlikely to be met if all parties – teachers, pupils, heads, governors and parents – are not involved in some way in devising them and taking responsibility for their achievement. It is crucial for governors to ask about the levels of involvement of the various parties in the setting of targets because without such 'ownership' the chances of success will be slim. For example, have the pupils been involved in negotiating their own targets with their teachers, and have the parents been informed of these and how they might assist in their achievement?

A discussion of targets and progress towards them – a regular item on the governing body's agenda perhaps – helps to show clearly what the school, group or individual is aiming at. Target-setting will take place on a number of levels – national, local, school and departmental – but ultimately it should affect individual pupils. Periodically, governors might want to ask the question: 'How is the meeting of this target going to help raise pupil achievement or improve teaching and learning in the school?'

Stage 4: What must we do to make it happen? Planning for action

After the audit has been completed and targets for improvement have been set, the planning process can begin, during which governors and staff together will be able to discuss the development priorities. As well as the areas for improvement identified by them, there will usually be other issues imposed or suggested by external agencies that require attention. There has also to be a balance between 'maintenance' and 'development'. Not all of the school's available resources can be put into improvement; there will be areas of the school that will require resourcing in order to maintain their present level of success and these must not be neglected. The purpose of Development Planning is to identify where the priorities lie so that appropriate resources, whether of money, staff or time, can be allocated to them. Unless there is clear identification of priorities it is possible that the resources will be spread so thinly across all areas that it becomes impossible for significant improvement to occur anywhere; if everything is a priority then nothing is!

During the stage of *action planning* the school revises its existing plans (the SDP or SIP and, where appropriate, the post-OFSTED action plan) to highlight the action that is required to achieve the agreed targets. As noted earlier, the targets need to be a central part of the school's plans. The individual actions can then be carefully planned with details provided about who is responsible for what, the time-scale by which the targets will be reached, resource and staff development implications and the success criteria and outcomes that will be achieved.

As we show below and elsewhere in the book, schools and governors have had some experience of the planning process – School Development Plans and post-OFSTED action plans are found in virtually all schools. With all plans the key to success is to translate the priorities identified in the plan into *effective action*. Many schools have already successfully integrated their post-OFSTED action plans with their Development Plans. Governors and senior staff now need to consider how target-setting will also be integrated. When the plans are next reviewed some priorities may need to change to reflect the targets set. It may, for example, only involve some fine-tuning to ensure that the SDP's success criteria are clear and expressed in terms of targets, particularly performance outcome targets.

Action planning for target-setting – the fourth stage in the cycle – involves identifying:

- a timetable for action;
- who will be responsible for ensuring the action takes place;
- what success will look like;
- what support and resources will be needed.

Target-setting does not necessarily mean 'more' resources but it might mean redirecting resources. It is relatively easy to set targets but how will they be achieved? The key lies in what happens at classroom level and governors need to ask of the school:

- What do we stop doing?
- What do we start doing?
- What do we keep on doing?

The governing body also needs to be aware that targets will have an effect on the system and therefore ensure that any ensuing changes are for the benefit of *all* pupils. Governors will have an important role in this stage of the cycle to make sure that all of the above are given proper consideration, particularly the strategies and approaches to be adopted and the resource implications of the targets set. In this way it should be clear to all parties '*what must be done to make it happen*'.

Stage 5: Taking action and reviewing progress. Making it happen

This is the most important stage in the target-setting cycle as the school brings about the desired changes and restarts the cycle of improvement. If the four preceding stages of the cycle take up ten months of the year and leave just two months for action, then the cycle has failed. Of course there is a need to discuss, analyse and agree on targets, which will take time for it to be done thoroughly, but if it is to the detriment of *making it happen* it will not be time well spent. Translating the agreed plan into action will be very much a matter for the staff, though governors can usefully be involved in monitoring progress towards the achievement of the goals (see the next chapter). Setting the success criteria during the planning stage is the key to good evaluation and details of the monitoring and evaluation processes should be built into the plan. Periodical review and monitoring will show if the changes are having the desired effect. How the targets will be monitored should be carefully considered and governors may agree with the professionals to be involved in the process either directly (e.g. by working with staff collecting evidence, visiting classrooms, talking with parents) or indirectly (e.g. by ensuring that progress on targets is a regular item on the governing body's agenda). In some cases it may be agreed to set up a small working party of governors and staff with the specific brief of monitoring and reviewing progress. At the very least, the governing body should receive regular reports on progress throughout the year and should evaluate the overall success of the plan before the planning cycle begins again. Regular monitoring may show better than expected progress to date and the need to revise the targets the school has set itself. By heads and governors *taking action and reviewing progress* in this way the school comes full circle and returns to Stage 1 of the target-setting cycle.

Vignette 5.1   *The involvement of the governing body of a junior school in development planning*

The head and chair of a junior school have been concerned for some time about the format of their SDP and how it was produced – the 'ownership' of the document. They believe that it is important for staff and governors to be involved in the planning process rather than just to receive a finished document. The head and chair had together attended a management course aimed at governors and senior staff and, as a result of their attendance at this course they decided to revisit the SDP.

Questionnaires were distributed to every member of staff, and, once completed, they were analysed by the deputy head. The staff appeared generally satisfied with this procedure: 'The staff feel that they have their say – what the staff say is seen as important by the governors' (Teacher-governor). Following the analysis of staff views by the deputy, the head then drew up a draft of the SDP that was presented to a group of governors. Due to a shortage of time the first draft was distributed at the meeting of the group of governors rather than in advance. Some of the governors made adverse comments on the draft; and the head, while understanding the criticisms at a rational level, felt painfully and personally affronted by them. The chair was concerned about the effect of these comments on the head at a difficult time and so took over the first draft and presented a revised plan to the next meeting of the full governing body. As the head didn't appear to 'own' this version, the governors 'felt they could wade in and have a real go' and there was a very full discussion of the ideas embodied in the plan. The head and chair believe that the questioning process is all-important: 'Previously we've been asking the wrong questions' (Head); 'The questions you ask shape what happens' (Chair); 'Ask not "Have you got any ideas?" but rather "What are the needs of the school?" How will this make a difference to the children's learning?' (Head).

The head and chair feel that sharing the task with the rest of the governors has enabled them to move towards a framework that feels more comfortable and within which both staff and governors can contribute more easily. Governors have since told the chair that they felt they had their hands on the plan and that looking at the basic document had been much more enriching. The SDP is a working document for both governors and staff and is frequently referred to: 'Our current SDP is the best we've had. Last year's was more airy-fairy and the one before that was too bland' (Governor); 'One of the governors has given a new approach and helped us to sharpen up our success criteria' (Teacher-governor).

Vignette 5.2   Governors' initial involvement in setting curriculum targets

As stated earlier, since September 1998 all governing bodies are required to ensure targets are set and published for pupil performance in the core subjects of English and Maths, and in GCSEs. Governors had therefore to accustom themselves to new concepts and to a new task. The experience of the governors of a junior, infant and nursery school when approaching this new responsibility was not untypical. All governors were members of the Curriculum Committee and they began their consideration of target-setting with a presentation by an LEA adviser. The issues raised by governors in discussion included:

- A possible sacrifice in breadth in the curriculum in return for a concentration on literacy and numeracy: 'You can get a wonderful set of results but a poorer product' (Governor).
- The possible neglect of some children (able and less able) in order to concentrate on those who are on the borderline and whose performance might be improved sufficiently in order to achieve the required standard: 'I want improvement for all children' (Governor).
- The implications for teachers' workload/resources/the SDP.
- Is the national or LEA target really attainable?
- What will be the parental view, for example of schools that set low targets/fail to achieve their targets? How will parents react when told that their child is in a year group of below-average ability?

Issues arising from the vignettes

A key issue in planning – whether it is a strategic plan, the Development/Improvement Plan or a post-OFSTED action plan (see Chapter 7) – is its ownership. Governors are unlikely to feel that they own a plan that has been presented to them only in its final draft and they may be reluctant to offer criticism or commentary on a plan that is clearly already the result of much hard work by the teachers. In such a situation it is realistically almost impossible for them to make any meaningful contribution. Governors should have the chance to be involved in setting the broad parameters before the detailed work begins. A key role for governors at all stages of the planning process is to ask questions: 'Why are you suggesting this? What about ... ? Why don't we ... ?' Governors need to be assisted and encouraged by the professionals in this process of asking the right questions. Individual governors may well have experience of planning gained through their own employment. This experience can be shared with the governors and staff in order to improve the planning process. The involvement of governors helps to promote a stronger sense of partnership between the governing body and the staff.

As with other forms of planning, governing bodies must decide for themselves, after discussion with school senior staff, what their level of involvement in the setting of targets should be. For the curriculum and pupil performance targets it is important for governors to take into account the advice of the head and the views of the staff. These discussions, however, need to be informed by the statutory requirement that governing bodies, in conjunction with their schools, must ensure that targets are set. Pupil performance targets have to be set in the core National Curriculum subjects of Maths and English, and (for the secondary sector) in public examinations (GCSEs). It is also a legal requirement that progress on meeting these agreed targets is reported at the annual parents' meeting held by the governing body.

In some schools, governors and staff, particularly as they become more capable and comfortable with the target-setting process, will want to go beyond this statutory minimum and set targets for other aspects of pupil achievement. This may include, for example, a wide range of pupil outcomes (e.g. participation in extra-curricular activities, attitudes to school, self-esteem, etc.). In this way schools, governing bodies and parents are able to set targets centred on those things they most value and which are consonant with their own aims.

Conclusion

The SDP/SIP is the all-important link between the school's vision as expressed in its long-term strategic plan and day-to-day improvement in the classroom. It provides an opportunity for governors and staff to work together in the management of their school, giving a sense of a shared vision and joint ownership. Working together on the plan helps to enhance the governor–teacher partnership and offers the governors a chance to contribute, directly or indirectly, to improvement within their school. Governors, when considering the school's budget and INSET planning, can help to ensure that these are linked to the priorities identified in the SDP, which includes targets and success criteria, and well-defined monitoring and evaluation strategies. Above all, Improvement or

Development Plans focus on teaching and learning, and improving pupil outcomes.

Effective target-setting, linked to the school's planning process, can help raise expectations and sharpen the focus on what pupils are learning and the impact of teaching on attainment. Through effective planning and target-setting, governing bodies, working closely with senior staff, are able to maintain and improve the standards of achievement in their schools. As with the other planning mechanisms found in schools, with experience, target-setting should become easier to carry out. The chances of success, however, will be greater if heads and governors are aware of some of the factors that make for effective target-setting. Target-setting should not be confined to pupils; there is no reason why target-setting should not also apply to school performance generally, including the performance and development of teachers, of subject departments and, of course, governing bodies. A growing number of governing bodies are already setting improvement targets for themselves. After all, if teachers and pupils are being asked to achieve set targets, then why not governors too? Governors might want to ask themselves if the way they operate allows them to focus on making their school more effective. Do they use their limited time to good effect and do the actions of the governing body 'make a difference'? If they don't, perhaps appropriate targets should be set for improvement.

Where Development Planning is a shared activity between staff and governors, it enhances the sense of partnership between them. Governors who abdicate their role in the production of the school's Development Plan are missing one of their best opportunities to contribute to school improvement. Having a governors' Development Plan within the overall SDP can demonstrate their commitment to improvement in their schools and emphasises the point that this is an activity in which they share with the staff. Plans should include details of how progress is to be monitored and governors can share in the monitoring in a variety of ways. At one level, if they are aware of the priorities set out in the plan, they can bear these in mind when visiting the school and look for evidence of the plan in action. Also they might be involved more formally in any arrangements for monitoring (see Chapter 6). At the very least, the Development or Improvement plan should be an agenda item for a full governors' meeting once a term when the head, and other members of staff as appropriate, can report on progress. A possible 'way in' for the governors to the planning cycle is for them to become involved in the evaluation phase. They may then find it easier to contribute ideas when priorities for the coming year are being discussed. The statutory requirement for governing bodies to ensure the school has set targets provides yet another entrée.

Target-setting and Improvement Planning: questions for consideration

1   How will the audit of the school's present position be conducted? Who will be involved and what data are to be collected?
2   Is good use being made of the available benchmarking data?
3   How do we ensure that our targets are 'SMART' and include a wide range of pupil outcomes? How do we ensure 'ownership' of the targets? Will any of the targets relate specifically to the governing body?
4   How will the priorities for improvement be chosen and who will be involved in the discussion? Are our targets an integral part of the Improvement Plan?
5   How do we ensure that the fifth stage of the improvement cycle – taking action and reviewing progress – is given sufficient priority?
6   How will progress towards the achievement of the chosen goals be monitored?
7   What are the arrangements for keeping the governing body informed of progress?
8   How will the effects of the plan at the end of the year be evaluated?
9   How do we ensure that any factors inhibiting improvement are removed or, at least, their influence minimised?
10 Above all, how do we ensure that we maintain our focus on raising standards and enhancing quality?

Chapter 6

Governors' role in review, evaluation and monitoring

Introduction

The second of the governing body's three main roles is to act as a critical friend to the school: 'Critical in the sense of its responsibility for *monitoring and evaluating* the school's effectiveness, asking challenging questions and pressing for improvement' (DFE/BIS/OFSTED 1995: 2, our italics). It is worth a moment's reflection to consider what the phrase 'critical friend' implies. A friend is trusted and fully understands the situation in which one finds oneself and what one is attempting to achieve in that context. From that basis of understanding, the critical friend is able to ask provocative and probing questions, provide data to be examined through another lens, and offer critique of a person's work while being an advocate for the success of that work (Costa and Kallick 1993). Such a definition places considerable demands on both governors and staff. Trust is not easily achieved – it takes time to develop and the governors have to be prepared to commit the time to understand the context in which the teachers are working as well as what they are trying to achieve. There are very significant implications for the governor–teacher relationship and the knowledge that governors have of their schools if they are to be able to act as critical friends.

Monitoring is, broadly speaking, the process of keeping a watch or checking on the progress on some aspect of the school's performance, or as a new scheme unfolds to ensure that plans and intentions are underway; asking the question 'are we carrying out our plans?' Thus governors might *monitor* pupil attendance over the year through a pattern of regular reports given to them in order to judge the success of a new school policy aimed at improving attendance. Whereas monitoring is an ongoing process, evaluation takes place towards the end of a programme or after a new policy has been in place for a set period. The question being asked here is 'Were the outcomes worthwhile?' Evaluation involves the collection and analysis of data in order to form a judgement about the value or worth of an activity. Thus the governors might *evaluate* the success of the new strategy designed to improve pupil attendance after one year against the success criteria that were established when the scheme was introduced before deciding whether or not to continue with the new policy. The term *review* is usually used to describe the process of making a judgement about policy, using evaluation data to inform decisions for strategic planning.

Governors should beware, however, of concentrating upon easily collected statistics – examination and test results, attendance rates, etc. Important though these are, they only provide part of the jigsaw of effectiveness. We must all learn to measure what we value in education and not simply value what we can easily measure.

Governors' role in monitoring

Monitoring progress – that is, checking on progress towards the desired outcomes – is an important aspect of the Development Planning cycle; an aspect that is all too easily overlooked. *Lessons in Teamwork*, a booklet published jointly by the Audit Commission and OFSTED in 1995, includes the governing body's monitoring role as one of five aspects of its work: 'making sure that the school adheres to its policies, budgets and plans; keeping informed about the quality and standards of education in the school, including pupil achievement' (Audit Commission/OFSTED 1995: 4). The school should have a programme by which progress is monitored regularly and systematically. Every innovation or target should have specific and precise criteria by which its success may be determined. It has to be said that, in the heady days of widespread curriculum innovation in the 1960s, monitoring and evaluation were areas that schools generally neglected. Not only were the success of the innovations rarely evaluated but there were often no clear success criteria against which to judge their success.

Governors can support monitoring and evaluation in their schools by being involved in the process either individually or collectively and by contributing to the co-ordination of the programme of monitoring (OCEA Partnership 1997). Monitoring and evaluation require time and any action that is to be taken as a result of the outcomes of evaluation will almost certainly require resources, perhaps in the form of further staff development, books and equipment for pupils, etc. Governors should ensure action *is* taken after evaluation and that both the monitoring/evaluation processes themselves and any consequent actions are properly resourced.

Monitoring should be an ongoing process within the school. Evidence can be gathered from a variety of sources:

- the professional views of teachers (individually and/or in groups) and other professionals connected with the school;
- the views and opinions of others, e.g. pupils, parents, local employers;
- the observation of pupils and/or the examination of samples of their work;
- the results of formal assessments of pupils: SATs, GCSEs, etc.;
- the study of documentation produced by the school, e.g. policy statements, schemes of work, communications to parents, etc.;

- statistics collected by the school, e.g. on attendance, exclusions, number of pupils with statements of special educational needs, etc.

Much of this data will already be in existence in the school and will merely need collating. Other information will have to be collected and this takes time, and governors may well be able, as the examples below illustrate, to assist staff in the collection process. To be able to monitor effectively, governors must know and understand what the school is trying to achieve. Data or information, in itself, is not an answer; it is merely a starting point from which one can start to ask appropriate questions. Governing bodies have a responsibility for monitoring School Development Plans and post-OFSTED action plans, the school's finances, the implementation of school policies and the quality of education provided. To do this effectively, governors require not only information but also the ability to interpret and analyse that information. Governors need to be able to go beyond the data to what is actually happening in the classrooms.

Vignette 6.1   The involvement of governors in reviewing the work of a secondary school department

A secondary school at which the GCSE results have shown a steady improvement in recent years has operated a system of departmental reviews since 1991 but in the early days there was no governor involvement in the process. Ideally, the work of each department is reviewed by the senior management of the school every two years. The review is spread out over a week and typically involves the observation of some fourteen or fifteen lessons by the review team, discussions with staff and the examination of documentation and samples of pupils' work provided by the department. Before the review takes place, the head of department concerned is invited to identify any preferred focal points for the review.

Once the review has been completed, verbal feedback is first offered to the head of department who then has the opportunity to comment upon and to correct any factual errors in the first draft of the written report before this is circulated to and discussed by the whole department. The full written report on the department is not presented to governors although the governor who is linked to the department will normally use this as a basis for his or her termly report to the governing body. An overview of the review is also presented to the governors' Curriculum Committee.

As the review process has developed since its inception, there has been a greater emphasis on the identification of areas for development and improvement. There has also been a greater degree of involvement from middle management within the school. As the process has been refined, so the team involved has been enlarged. The team now involved in a review is as follows:

- the three members of the senior management team;

- the head of another faculty;
- the governor linked to the department;
- possibly the appropriate LEA adviser.

The inclusion of a head of faculty in the team provides an element of 'peer appraisal' but is also seen as part of the professional development of that individual. The involvement of governors in the review process came about through the governors' expressed desire to become more involved in curricular issues. Joining in the reviews was seen as one way of facilitating this. Usually, but not invariably, the governor involved in the review is the governor linked to the department, though one governor has expressed concern about the difficulties of remaining objective when he or she already knows the members of the department well. The governors are able to bring a different perspective to the process. They are expected partly to play a similar role to that of the lay inspector in an OFSTED inspection and to comment from the point of view of what a parent might expect, i.e. adding the lay perspective to the professional view.

Ideally, the governor attends the pre-review meeting of the senior management team but in practice this has rarely been possible. When the governor is unable to attend this meeting, he or she is briefed by the headteacher on their role in the process. Typically, a governor will see a number of lessons from different teachers with pupils across the age and ability range. He or she will also interview a member of the department and/or the head of department. A governor might look, for instance, at pupil behaviour, the use of resources and continuity/differentiation, and his/her report might refer to matters such as the topics covered, the behaviour and response of the pupils to the teaching, resources and accommodation, and homework. Recently, the head of one, very successful, department asked that the review should explore the reasons for the differences in performance of boys and girls. The link governor, as well as observing lessons taught by three different teachers in which he focused particularly on the reactions of boys and girls, also interviewed a group of four boys and a group of four girls in an effort to explore possible differences of attitude towards the subject. The report on the review concluded that the most valuable aspect of the process was the time spent by the senior staff and the governor on interviewing pupils and a number of issues emerged as a result of these interviews.

There are a number of significant features about the review process:

- departmental reviews are one of a range of strategies directed towards school improvement;
- the process has clear aims and procedures that are known to all;
- the review process lasts for several days;
- members of the SMT are involved in the review;
- a head of department/faculty from another subject area is involved;

- a governor, usually the link governor, is involved for a full day;
- when appropriate, an LEA adviser is involved;
- during the review, lessons are observed, schemes of work and samples of pupils' work are studied and members of the department/faculty are interviewed;
- a written report is prepared at the end of the review with the head of department/faculty being invited to comment on the first draft.

Vignette 6.2   Governors' involvement in monitoring the work of a primary school

The governors' involvement in monitoring the work of the school has developed over the years and was the focus of a training day – 'The Role of the Governing Body: Monitoring Quality' – held on a Saturday (in November 1996). A system of formal and informal visiting had earlier been instituted that attempted to ensure all governors were able to gain knowledge and insights into the operation of the school. The governing body and staff were agreed that the best way for governors to get to know the school, the staff and the children was by visiting. However, it was also noted that 'governors are not appointed to check up on the professional work of the school, but to keep under review the way in which the school is working and developing' (Policy statement for governor visits, June 1995). Arrangements were made for governors to take part in planned school visits. All concerned knew the purpose and format of the visits. *Informal* visits – one per year, lasting from an hour to half a day – were expected to be undertaken by each member of the governing body although it was recognised that this was unlikely to be possible for all governors. A rota of visits was finalised at the last full governing body meeting at the end of each academic year and the focus of the informal visit might be a classroom, year group or a particular interest of the governor. (Each governor was given a personal planner to enter dates of meetings, training and school visits – both formal and informal.) Advice was given both before, during and after the informal visit, and for reporting back to the governors' Curriculum Committee.

The system of *formal* visits was more concerned with monitoring and took place each term, lasting a minimum of half a day. The focus of the formal visit was determined by the priorities in the School Development Plan, which were set by the management:

> they have made professional judgements about what needs to be done. ... [The governing body] do not set a separate agenda unless we were hearing some very worrying things but this has not happened. In context of the review we are monitoring the SDP.
>
> (Chair)

At the time of the research, the curriculum areas of Art, Mathematics,

English and Music had been covered as well as that of 'equal opportunities'. Two governors undertook the formal visit, one of whom was the curriculum link governor (all fifteen governors had a curriculum link), together with another governor, who could be a teacher-governor. ('Two pairs of eyes are better than one', as a governor said.) The school's curriculum co-ordinator was released at the time of the formal visit to accompany the visiting governors. (Supply cover was available for the duration of the visit and for the follow-up meeting.) This offered the governors access to the co-ordinator's expertise to inform their visit and to answer any questions that arose related to the focus area during the visit. It also enabled teachers to continue with their teaching while governors were in their classes.

The visiting governors met with the head and the relevant curriculum co-ordinator at least two weeks before the visit to:

- decide on the date of the visit;
- plan and discuss the aspects that they wish to consider;
- plan the timetable for the visit, who will be observed and when, etc.;
- receive all relevant documentation, policy statements, etc.

The co-ordinator then reported back to the staff to inform them of the planned timetable and format of the visit.

Advice was offered to visiting governors. For example, governors could look at recently purchased resources when the curriculum area under focus had received a significant input of funding as a result of the priority placed on it in the SDP. Governors were given the opportunity to consider and review value for money and the effective use of resources. The building was to be considered in terms of the quality of the environment and the relationships between staff and pupils, and between the children. Visiting governors were advised to stick to the timetable for the visit as staff would be expecting them at a certain time (and, it was noted, 'will almost certainly, have prepared their lesson on this basis'). Prearranged questions were mainly used but the co-ordinator could be asked any other questions that arose. Opportunities to talk to staff could be taken but questions asked that put staff at their ease. Visiting governors were encouraged to be positive in outlook and to check what was going on and the purpose of any activity, looking at pupils' work as appropriate. Above all the teacher's expertise had to be respected.

The head saw the governors' role as seeing the school at work and asking the right questions:

> what are the children doing, is it an exciting place, what's on the board? Is the learning environment good, is there a trusted environment where the children can take risks? Are they messing about because they are bored? Do the teachers really know their kids, and so on? This will give governors the

confidence that the school is a functioning well-oiled body that is giving the children a good education. But it comes back to asking questions like why is it that boys are not doing so well in Key Stage 1 and Key Stage 2 English and what are we doing about it? We are drip feeding the governors so they would be asking these kind of questions.

(Head)

After the visit, time was spent with the co-ordinator and/or head to talk about what had been seen and to discuss any further questions. This was an opportunity for governors to start considering what issues were to go in the final report. Observations were fed back at this point, with governors unafraid to express concerns or comment favourably on what they had seen. One of the governors would take responsibility to produce the first draft of the report, ensuring that no member of staff was named, while the other would report back at the next full governing body meeting. The draft report was seen by the head and the relevant co-ordinator and a meeting arranged about two weeks after the formal visit to discuss it.

When reporting back to the full governing body the co-ordinator concerned was invited to attend the meeting and could then answer any questions arising. Governors received a copy of the report in advance so were in a good position to discuss it with the two visiting governors, the head and the curriculum co-ordinator.

There was general support for these visits and staff commented on how helpful they had been: 'The governors are supportive, they come out with positive things and they know we're doing a good job. ... Formal visits are a way of saying well done' (Head). Also, 'Staff need to know that governors are not just making blind decisions – it helps overcome the "what do governors know – they never come into the school" syndrome' (Head). Governors found the visits positive, valuable and informative: 'I feel I now understand more about how Art is taught and how things are going in Art' (Chair).

The head saw the system of visiting as helpful and as a way of ensuring things got done:

It's not threatening but it does keeps us on our toes – in a healthy way – for deadlines which we have set. We set the targets and governors coming in to do their monitoring role make sure it is happening and from that as professionals we are evaluating – governors provide that lay view and ensure there are no gaps.

(Head)

The system was not without its problems and the chair expressed a concern:

I've done two formal visits this year – am I volunteering because no one else is? We need a better system to monitor who is doing it to ensure greater governor involvement. ... We have reviewed it recently and we need to keep it under review to ensure it is good use of everyone's time.

(Chair)

Through formal and informal visiting by governors it was felt that important decisions had a much better chance of being based on a knowledge of what was actually happening in the school, its curriculum and organisation. As a result of monitoring the work of the school in this way, governors had increased confidence in their ability to carry out their full responsibilities and to know that the school was doing everything possible to enhance the quality of teaching and learning.

Vignette 6.3   Governors' involvement in monitoring a special school

At one time, the governors at a special school for pupils with emotional and behavioural difficulties were linked to a class and to a curriculum area with the intention that governors would monitor work in these areas. However, the governors felt uncomfortable with the curriculum link and the system was not generally successful. The governors were concerned that, as lay people, they were unable to make judgements about educational issues: 'The governors didn't want the teachers to feel we were making judgements' (Chair). One of the difficulties for governors was how improvement was to be measured in a special school. During a pre-OFSTED review, advisers from the LEA drew attention to the fact that the curriculum was not being discussed at governors' meetings.

Following this review it was decided to set up a Curriculum Committee consisting of all of the governors. The teachers responsible for the different curriculum areas would make presentations to this group during which they would explain the aims and content of their subject area. Governors would be shown how the staff divided the National Curriculum subjects down into medium-term schemes of work and hence into individual learning programmes for each child. Following one such presentation there was a discussion among the governors of their experiences of visiting classrooms. Some of the governors expressed their concern about their lack of confidence in monitoring the curriculum and also the lack of opportunities for them to get into the school to carry out this work. There was also uncertainty as to how governors could report back on what they had seen to staff and to their fellow governors, particularly if the governor had not made notes during the visit. The deputy head tried to reassure the governors about what was expected of them: 'Is what you see in accordance with the school's policy? How does it relate to the overall aims of the school? What about classroom management – is each child being treated with respect?'

The chair then prepared some guidelines for governors' visits to classrooms in order to see the subject in action, following which they would report back to the governors' meeting. Prior to one such visit, the chair made arrangements to visit a class. She discussed her visit with the teacher beforehand, saw the resources available and was provided with a lesson plan. After she had observed the lesson, she spent some time in discussion with the teacher. Following her visit, the chair felt that she was aware of the curriculum for the subject that she had observed being taught and the associated schemes of work and that she had seen them being delivered in the classroom. During her visit she was also able to observe the school's 'Restraint and Handling' policy in operation when she saw a child having to be physically returned to her place.

Issues arising from the vignettes

Schools and their governing bodies are different: a pattern of monitoring that is appropriate in one school will not necessarily be right in a different situation. Clearly, in the examples above, the rather formal pattern of reviews that is highly effective in the secondary school might be quite 'over the top' in the primary and special schools. It is up to the governors and staff together to devise a pattern of monitoring, evaluation and review that suits their school and their circumstances. The degree to which governors are involved in the collection of evidence depends also on the area under review. Governors might, for instance, be directly involved in the evaluation of the school's Health and Safety policy or a curriculum review of the type described above but often it will be more likely that the governing body will be seeking answers from the professionals. Governors will want to be assured that monitoring is occurring.

There is a danger of governors having too great an involvement in day-to-day monitoring or trying to adopt an inspectorial role. Governors and teachers need to be clear about the purposes of the exercise, how evidence is to be gathered and how that evidence will be used. It may well be helpful to have some form of 'protocol' that covers these issues (OCEA Partnership 1997). It must also be remembered that the majority of governors are lay people with limited experience of educational practice and hence may not be in a position to be able to make informed (professional) judgements on teaching methods. Governors are, after all, lay people and their strength has always been seen in these terms.

Effective monitoring requires time and effort, sometimes in very considerable amounts, and governors should ensure that the exercise is providing value for money. The benefits, however, can be very significant, as indicated by the expected outcomes of the review described in Vignette 6.1. Involving governors in monitoring in this way requires that they must be able to devote sufficient time to the process. One has to recognise that it is not always easy for some governors to be able to spend a whole day or even a half-day in their school and it may be that only some are able to be fully involved in this way. In Vignette 6.2 the question of time was raised in a number of ways: time to undertake the formal and informal visits and whether or not the workload was being distributed equally between members of the governing body. Time spent on monitoring visits also included preparation time and report writing and feedback to the governing body, as well as the half-day or day spent in the school. Finally, it also included release time for the relevant co-ordinator to accompany the visiting governors while in school. The governing body had therefore to ensure that the benefits of the monitoring system warranted the time and resources they were devoting to it.

If all governors are not involved in monitoring there must be procedures through which all are kept informed. However, caution must be exercised when monitoring reveals a situation that might conceivably lead to disciplinary action being taken against a teacher for incompetence. If this occurs, governors on the appeals panel must not be brought into the discussions so that, if necessary, they could come to a hearing with no prior knowledge of the case.

Conclusion

Some governors believe that their role is limited to ensuring that there are mechanisms in place for monitoring in the school rather than being actually involved in the monitoring themselves. After all is that not what school managers are paid to do?: 'We need to know that the processes of planning and monitoring are in place' (Primary school governor). However, the Chief Inspector commented in a recent report (OFSTED 1998b) that governors are not 'sufficiently involved in monitoring or evaluating the effectiveness of their schools or the outcomes of their financial decisions' (par. 69). Secondary school governors were doing slightly better in this area but the governing bodies of special schools were only rarely involved in monitoring. A frequent criticism of schools identified by inspectors as having serious weaknesses was that governors were unaware of their school's performance in relation to other similar schools.

Monitoring, evaluation and review will not of themselves bring about improvement but they are an important part of the improvement process. Governors' involvement in a programme of systematic and regular monitoring can thus be seen as making a significant contribution to school improvement. While governors should not be attempting to act as inspectors – a task for which they generally have neither the inclination, the training nor the experience – neither should their visits to classrooms lack a focus. When governors go into a classroom with a clear idea of what they are looking for and what questions to ask, the visits are much more worthwhile for both governors and staff. Quite apart from the essential nature of monitoring as an aid to improvement, a joint approach to the task by governors and teachers enhances the nature of the partnership between them:

> Monitoring is one of the most positive ways in which the governing body, head and staff can work together. It is one of the most significant ways in

which all of these people can contribute effectively to the permanent interests of the school over time.

(OCEA 1997: 6)

Governors' involvement in monitoring and evaluation: questions for consideration

1   Does the school have a programme for the systematic and regular monitoring of progress?
2   Does the programme require further development?
3   Are governors actively involved in the monitoring process?
4   Could their involvement be usefully extended?
5   Is there a protocol that makes clear to all the purposes and methodology of the monitoring programme?
6   How are the results of the monitoring programme reported to governors?
7   Do all innovations have clear and precise criteria against which their success may be evaluated?

Chapter 7

The governing body and OFSTED inspections

Introduction

The Education (Schools) Act 1992 introduced a regime of systematic inspections of all state schools in England and Wales on a four-year (later extended to six-year) cycle. Prior to this, school inspections were relatively infrequent – Her Majesty's Inspectorate undertook between 100 and 150 each year and the amount of inspection undertaken by local education authorities was variable. Under the new arrangements inspections were to be managed by the Office for Standards in Education (OFSTED) according to a published Framework. Inspectors were required to undergo training, to pass a registration assessment and were contracted to carry out inspections after having a tender accepted by OFSTED. The inspection of schools by privatised teams commenced in the secondary sector in England and Wales in September 1993 and was introduced a year later into primary and special schools. All schools in England and Wales had been inspected by the summer of 1998.

School inspections had to follow a national Framework (OFSTED 1994a) that covers four main areas:

- the quality of education provided by the school;
- the standards achieved by the pupils;
- the management and efficiency of the use of resources;
- the spiritual, moral, social and cultural development of pupils.

It will be noted that these are the four areas specified for improvement in *Improving Schools* (OFSTED 1994b) to which we referred in Chapter 1.

Reasons for inspecting schools include the following:

- to ensure accountability – for quality, standards and use of resources, and the effective use of public funds;
- to provide information to parents, the local community, for local and national government;
- to monitor and assess the performance of schools;

- to assist in school improvement by identifying strengths and weaknesses, and the action needed to improve.

The official logo of OFSTED is 'Improvement through Inspection'. It is claimed that inspections provide a spur to improvement in two main ways:

- Schools are given a period of notice (usually two terms) before an inspection takes place. Schools can therefore prepare and undertake developmental and remedial measures with the intention of avoiding adverse comment in the following inspection.
- After inspection, the governing body is required to produce an action plan that addresses areas of weakness identified in the inspection report (Matthews and Smith 1995).

The role of the governing body in inspection

There is no shortage of advice and information for governors on what the inspection of the school will involve and the nature of the governing body's main responsibilities that may be appraised (e.g. O'Connor 1996; Stiles 1996). Many LEAs have produced guidance documents for governors and provided training, either for individual governors or for the whole governing body, on what inspection entails and what will be expected of governors both during and after the inspection. Some LEAs offer 'pre-inspection inspections' designed to help schools to prepare for the OFSTED inspection. How governing bodies are able to cope with and respond to the inspection process, before it occurs, during the actual inspection and afterwards, will differ depending on the demands made on the governing body and its level of collective competence. The balance between the demands made on the governors by the inspection process and their overall competence to respond accordingly has been conceptualised by one of the governor-training organisations (Institution for School and College Governors 1996) and their model is reproduced as Figure 7.1.

OFSTED inspection reports might usefully be able to categorise governing bodies in such terms. However, the range and extent of inspectors' comments regarding the operation of school governing bodies has been shown to vary considerably from one report to another (Creese 1997).

One important question to be asked is whether an OFSTED inspection should be seen as an inspection *of* the school including its governing body, or as being undertaken largely *for* the governing body? There is no clear cut answer to this question other than to say that elements of both are likely to apply. In terms of being *for* school and the governing body, the inspection process provides them with a comprehensive analysis or audit of the school's strengths and weaknesses. The immediate task of the governing body after the inspection is to attend the feedback session given by the Registered Inspector and then to work with the headteacher on the post-OFSTED action plan. Following an

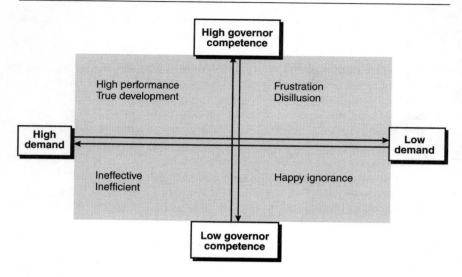

Figure 7.1 A model of the balance between governing body competence and the demands placed upon it

inspection, it is the responsibility of the school's governing body to devise an action plan that aims to address the 'key issues for action' identified by the inspectors. This plan should give a concise overview of proposed actions, iden-tify priorities, state what action is to be taken, set deadlines for targets to be met and identify the resources needed. The action plan should also indicate who is responsible for the particular actions, how progress will be monitored and how it fits in with the existing priorities of the school's Development Plan. Schools and governing bodies have approached this in different ways with the level of governor involvement varying considerably. The outcomes of the inspection – the report and the key issues for action – are an important source of evidence for governors about their school and provide an opportunity for them to become more closely involved in monitoring the quality of education provided by the school.

As to the inspection being *of* the governing body, the report of an OFSTED inspection of the school will refer to the work of the governing body, particu-larly under the section on 'Management and Administration'. The inspectors' report should include an evaluation of school leadership and management which indicates how well the governors, head and senior staff contribute to the quality of education provided by the school and the standards achieved by all of the children. The Framework for the inspection of schools states that the Registered Inspector's report should include 'an evaluation of the strategic management of the resources available to the school, including an assessment of the work of the governing body and appropriate staff' (OFSTED 1994a).

Similarly, the school is to be judged by the inspectors partly in terms of the leadership shown by the governing body and whether effective working relationships exist so that common goals can be achieved. In addition the OFSTED handbook notes that the inspectors' report should also include 'an evaluation of the effectiveness of the governing body in fulfilling its legal responsibilities' (OFSTED 1994a).

Inspectors' comments on the governing body have varied in the detail given and perhaps for this reason OFSTED announced that for the spring term, 1998 – and for this term only – there would be a specific comment upon the performance of the governing body in one area. Governing bodies were to be graded by the inspectors on a seven-point scale in relation to the degree to which they were fulfilling their strategic role – in Gann's view the only effective role that a predominantly lay group of people can play in schools (1998). Inspectors were given no formal guidance from OFSTED on exactly how they should make their judgements, although broad criteria were offered for the achievement of grades 2, 4 and 6 (OFSTED, Update, 1997).

According to OFSTED, an analysis of the inspectors' grades of all 2,360 schools inspected in the spring term, 1998, shows that three-quarters of their governing bodies were 'satisfactory' or better, with secondary school governing bodies emerging as slightly better in the area of self-review than primary school governing bodies. Similarly, the recently published DfEE report on *Improving the Effectiveness of School Governing Bodies* uses inspection evidence of both schools and their governing bodies to point to the link between effective schools and effective governing bodies (Scanlon *et al.* 1999). What the researchers were unable to do, however, was to ascertain the direction of the causal link between the two. It will be interesting to see the long-term effects of the overall judgements of OFSTED inspectors on the performance of governing bodies. Already it is becoming clear that inspection has led to governors becoming both more involved in their schools and more aware of their responsibilities (Earley 1998).

There is some evidence, however, that inspection reports are rarely overtly critical of the governing body, even when the school is clearly in some difficulties (Creese 1997). A detailed analysis of references to governors in inspection reports, following up an earlier analysis (Creese 1994), found that the situation had changed very little, with much variation in practice. The governors in the more recent survey were very much more involved in providing evidence on which inspectors based their judgements. Evidence was likely to be derived from interviews – probably undertaken by the lay inspector and usually with the chair and/or the chairs of committees. The main finding of the study was that there was still considerable variation in the length and detail of the section of the report devoted to the work of the governing body, although it was noted that there is a greater consistency in inspectors' expectations regarding governors' roles and the way in which an effective governing body should operate. There were now a sufficient number of common themes and phrases running through the reports to suggest that a clearer view of what is expected of an effective governing body was now emerging from OFSTED. Creese suggests that OFSTED reports, in order to recognise adequately the commitment made by governors, should include at least one paragraph reporting on the work of the governing body.

After the immediate euphoria, relief and celebration of 'having survived OFSTED' the notion of a period of 'post-OFSTED' blues or depression, frequently followed by a dip in performance, has been noted. Not only does the governing body need to be aware of a possible dip in performance (which research suggests may last weeks, months or even terms – see Ferguson *et al.* 1999) but also it needs to be 'ready to suggest strategies to deal with staff morale and absence, pupil unrest, lack of energy for initiatives and so forth' (Institution for School and College Governors 1996). One of the most immediate tasks of all governing bodies after an inspection, regardless of the outcome, is to provide support for staff who invariably find the inspection process stressful. The task of remotivating and re-energising is likely to fall mainly on the shoulders of heads and senior staff who, in turn, often looked to the governing body to provide the necessary support and to approve the resources to enable the school to progress. This may take the form of approving spending on training or simply being available to talk with staff as and when needed. With the help of the LEA or Diocesan Board, for example, it may be found helpful to conduct a training needs analysis of the staff and to undertake an audit of the governing body. In this way it becomes clear what are the main areas that need to be addressed for progress to be made.

The post-OFSTED action plan

Governing bodies have played an important part in their schools' achievements following inspection. The inspection process has made many governing bodies give serious thought to the way in which they are operating. As noted in Chapter 5, the action plan should state very clearly and precisely how the governing body will address the key issues for action identified by the inspectors. It provides a unique opportunity for governors to be fully involved in the school. However, research conducted with a random sample of schools inspected in 1993 (few of which 'failed') found that almost half of the respondents (headteachers) thought that their governors had played little or no part in the creation of the post-OFSTED action plan (Ouston *et al.* 1996). More recent surveys of schools inspected in 1994 and 1996 found evidence of greater involvement. In 1996, for example, only 28 per cent of heads reported governors playing a minor role, while one-quarter reported them making a major contribution (Earley 1998).

Some schools found it helpful to form small subcommittees or working parties to guide the development of the post-OFSTED action plan or to work on individual key issues. These groups, which met regularly, usually involved both governors and staff as they provided excellent opportunities for all parties to work together and address the key issues facing the school. In other schools governors may be involved in the whole process – although not all were involved in everything – from the formulation of the draft plan to the monitoring of progress on individual key issues for action. In such situations, governors need to balance their involvement in the detail of the action plan against the need to maintain an overview that allows the governing body the perspective to prioritise and to view the plan with a necessary element of detachment.

Research shows that the process of producing and monitoring the action plan results in governing bodies beginning to act in new ways. They often become more directly involved in curriculum matters and the raising of standards. In some schools, for example, governors had attached themselves to particular school departments or curriculum areas, or they had taken part in staff appointments and school visits, and had given presentations (with the relevant teacher) to the whole governing body. Attempts were being made in a variety of ways and with the active support of heads, for the governing body to become better informed about the school and all its workings. This often meant, for both staff and governors, a change of *culture* (or 'the way things are done around here') to which some were said to have adjusted better than others. Governors were said to be more aware of how they could influence events and there was a greater willingness for them 'to get their hands dirty'. Governors needed to get to know their schools and be aware of what was being asked of teachers, particularly in terms of the day-to-day delivery of the curriculum. Greater first-hand experience of schools was said to enhance the partnership between teachers and the governing body, and ensure greater appreciation, mutual understanding and trust.

Governing bodies and 'failing' schools

This section, although focusing on what we know about schools that have 'failed' their inspection, has much relevance for *all* governing bodies as there are important lessons to be learned from the experience of these schools. Between September 1993 and the end of the first round of inspection (July 1998) about 700 schools (3 per cent) were identified as 'in need of special measures' – or as 'failing' schools. Fifty-four have closed and a small number – forty by the end of the 1997–8 school year – had made sufficient progress to be removed from the special measures register. Evidence from schools that 'failed' the inspection shows that their governing bodies have become more effective, making better use of the limited time available to them and assisting their schools to come off the special measures register (DfEE 1997e; Earley 1997; OFSTED 1997).

Understandably, 'failing' schools are not keen to dwell on the past but wish to stress the future and to emphasise where the school is going; not where it has been. There is little point in agonizing over the inspection process and the negativity surrounding the school's failings. It is more important to stress that the inspection had provided the school with a useful audit so that there is now a better understanding of what has to be done in order for the school to improve. Governing bodies of 'failing' schools were usually, on their own admission, not operating particularly effectively; the focus of their attentions had rarely, if ever, centred on the standards achieved by pupils and many were only partly fulfilling their roles and responsibilities. They were often operating as they had before the 1986 and 1988 Education Acts (which increased the range of governing body responsibilities), seeing their role – or having it defined for them – largely in traditional terms of attending school functions and endorsing or rubber-stamping the decisions of the head. Other governors felt that they had been prevented from fulfilling their roles and responsibilities; they saw themselves as having nothing to do.

The experience of being deemed a 'failing' school usually had devastating effects on both staff and pupils, particularly on their self-esteem. Individuals felt bruised, hurt and unvalued, and there was often a major job to be done of re-motivating the school community. The stresses and strains continued as HMI (usually two or three at a time) embarked upon regular (at least termly) monitoring visits to talk to heads and observe teaching and learning. Research shows that at most 'failing' schools a small number of staff leave; some voluntarily, while others had to be persuaded to leave or were subject to capability procedures. In some cases the issue of poor performance was easily and speedily resolved; in others it led to the instigation of formal capability or competence proceedings, which took some time to resolve.

It was usual for the DfEE and HMI to meet with the school and LEA shortly before the action plan was dispatched in order to explain the special measure arrangements and to offer informal comments on the draft plan. The most common criticism of draft plans centred on the inadequate arrangements for monitoring and evaluation. While the school was under special measures the action plan was likely to replace the School Development Plan (SDP) – where one existed. When the school came off the register the new action plan (which had to be produced following the HMI's report that special measures were no longer required) was usually incorporated into the SDP. Governors needed to make decisions about the issues to be given priority in any plans.

Legislation gives the LEA or the Diocesan Board, acting as the appropriate appointing authority, additional powers to help support schools in need of special measures. (These powers do not apply to schools with serious weaknesses.) The LEA has the power to suspend the school's right to a delegated budget and to appoint a small number of additional governors to the governing body. A governing body of a 'failing school' may decide that the time is right to take stock of the issues raised by the inspection, to compare these with its existing expertise and to suggest to the LEA or the Diocesan Board that it helps find additional governors with the kind of expertise that is needed. Indeed, most special measure schools have made changes to the composition of the governing body. LEAs and

Diocesan Boards often used their powers to appoint additional governors, bringing in people from a variety of backgrounds who they felt would make the governing body more effective. Headteachers and chairs of governors may also actively seek new recruits to add expertise to the governing body or to fill vacancies.

Other examples of forms of assistance offered by LEAs include additional resources (in some cases schools are allowed to spend over budget for a short period), advisers or co-ordinators being attached to schools or seconded senior staff made available. LEAs and Diocesan Boards are able to offer governing bodies additional training, particularly around issues of their own effectiveness that may have been flagged-up by the inspectors. This training can be delivered by LEAs themselves or by others. The LEA or the Diocesan Board may provide support, for example in the form of a clerk who, along with the link adviser, can provide an important source of professional expertise to the head and governing body, as well as being a link to the LEA or the Board.

Governing bodies of failing schools found that they had to become more effective, make better use of their limited time and assist their schools to come off the special measures register. Governors rarely directly affect the learning experiences of pupils; indirectly however there are many ways that governing bodies are able to influence those experiences and help raise standards of achievement. By acting in this manner governing bodies of all schools should be able to play an important role in ensuring that their schools never require special measures and that they continue to develop and improve.

We include here three vignettes illustrating the reaction of the school's governing body following its OFSTED inspection. Although two of these schools were identified as being in need of special measures to improve, we believe that there are important lessons to be learnt by all schools from the experiences of these two.

Vignette 7.1   The involvement of the governing body in post-OFSTED action planning

Following the OFSTED inspection of this junior school, the governors set up a small subgroup to prepare their action plan. The group consisted of the chair and vice-chair, the chairs of the Curriculum, Finance, Personnel and Site and Environment Committees, and the headteacher. Altogether, the group spent about six hours working on the draft action plan and the revised version was then circulated amongst the members of the group for further comments before the final draft was submitted to the full governing body for approval. The governors involved in the working group took their role very seriously and were keen to ensure that the school obtained the maximum benefit from the exercise: 'It's our job to make this a useful experience – we are committed to using the OFSTED report to move the school forward' (Chair). They were also anxious to ensure that the action taken would improve the quality of the pupils' education and there was an emphasis on appropriate staff development.

The initial draft prepared by the headteacher was examined in detail and the governors were concerned throughout to understand and address the 'key issues for action' as set out in the OFSTED report. They were determined to make the targets set as precise as possible and to ensure that adequate arrangements for monitoring and evaluation would be in place: 'How do we monitor this?' (Governor); 'How do we know this is being achieved?' (Governor). Throughout, it was a shared enterprise between the head and the governors; the head was very keen to ensure that the governors should feel that it was *their* plan: 'I hope that you feel that it's your action plan' (Head).

Vignette 7.2   The reaction of governors in a junior school identified 'as in need of special measures to improve'

Following an unfavourable report by a team of OFSTED inspectors in September 1994, a team of HMI visited the school in October/November 1995. They reported that there had been insufficient progress since the earlier inspection and that the school was in need of special measures in order to improve the standards of pupils' attainment and the quality of the teaching. The HMI report was not uncritical of the work of the governing body:

> The action plan has been a prominent feature of the governing body's meetings and governors have been keen to ensure that the school does what it can to bring about the necessary improvement. Their attention has, however, been on the simple execution of the various well-intentioned tasks rather than on their impact on standards and the quality of provision. The school should adopt a more strategic, rigorous approach to the construction and implementation of future plans.
>
> (par. 24)

Following the HMI report, the headteacher took early retirement and the head of a school elsewhere in the LEA was invited to become acting head. The governing body became more interventionist. Morale amongst the staff improved considerably with both staff and governors recognising that the role of the governing body had changed: 'A governor's role has changed from a rather benevolent side-liner to one which needs some positive input' (Governor); 'In the past the governors have taken a less active role than they do now' (Teacher). The governors recognised the importance of good relationships with the staff and involved themselves in an 'adopt-a-class scheme' whereby each member of the governing body was linked to a specific class and its teacher. One of the criticisms made by HMI was that there was insufficient monitoring and evaluation, and that there were no success criteria. The governors set up a monitoring group that meets regularly and consists of the chair, the head, two teachers (including the teacher-governor) and two governors.

One question remained unanswered. Could the governors in some way have prevented what happened?: 'I honestly thought when I came in that this was a good school – it felt good and there was a good working atmosphere' (Governor). The governors relied upon the advice of the then headteacher and the comments of the LEA officers and advisers. It is very difficult to see how they could have done otherwise:

> With hindsight, it is possible to see mistakes that were made in the past and how these pitfalls can be avoided. A firm foundation has been prepared for mutual trust between the governors and all of the staff at the school.
>
> (Governor)

Vignette 7.3   The reaction of the governors of a secondary school 'in need of special measures to improve'

The school is situated on the edge of a large city, serving an area of considerable social deprivation. Pupils enter the school with reading ages up to two years behind their chronological ages and there is little support from parents for the school – there is no PTA and not one parent, other than the parent-governors, attended the annual meeting between governors and parents in 1995: 'We are not a comprehensive school. We "lose" children to GM schools and we take on pupils excluded from the GM and LEA single-sex schools' (Teacher-governor). There is a history of a shortage of LEA-appointed governors and those appointed have often lacked interest in, and commitment to, the school.

The school was inspected by a team of OFSTED inspectors in early 1994 and received a not unfavourable report from them. However, a team of HMI visited the school one year later, their visit apparently being triggered by the school's poor showing in the 'league table' of examination results and attendance rates. HMI decided that the school required special measures to improve in spite of the fact that, if the school's results are considered in terms of 'value-added', the performance is very creditable. The school was one of the first in the country to be identified in this way and it came as a shock to the governors and staff: 'The governors were devastated' (Governor).

The school was originally a secondary modern school and at that time the governing body met only once a term and appears to have played little part in the life of the school. Attendance at meetings was not high. More recently, however, a core of strong, competent and committed governors emerged. The involvement and support of this core group of governors has been a very significant development in the school over the last two or three years. The HMI report appears to have had two very significant effects upon the governing body. First, the governing body, helped by the participation of a consultant appointed by the LEA, works together much more closely as a team: 'We spent more time together so we got to know one another better' (Governor); 'We worked more as a team' (Governor). Second, governors now visit the school very much more frequently: 'Before, we didn't see governors in school. They were happy to let the school carry on' (Teacher-governor). More frequent visiting by governors has strengthened the governor–teacher relationship and increased governors' confidence: 'Staff know now that they have the support of the governors – it's a team now – staff and governors' (Teacher-governor); 'Governors' confidence has grown a lot because they are in and out of the school so frequently. They must be getting a better view of what's going on in school' (Teacher-governor). As governors' confidence has grown, so their role has changed and developed: 'HMI have made the governing body a proper governing body, whereas before they were just a rubber stamp' (Teacher-governor). The governors now appear to appreciate that as one governor expressed it: 'They are there to provide strategic management and direction for the school.'

One of the points made by HMI was the need to increase governor participation in school policy-making and review. The governing body now meets at least twice a term. In addition to the Finance Committee there is also an Action Plan Monitoring and Evaluation Group (APMEG). Named governors are responsible for overseeing progress towards each target set out in the post-OFSTED action plan and each of them reports back regularly to the APMEG, which in turn reports to the full governing body. The monitoring has included pupil-shadowing and the study by governors of samples of pupils' work. The governors are now linked to departments within the school and are encouraged to visit their departments on a regular basis. Some of the governors are able to visit the school frequently, involving themselves in a range of matters including the production of the governors' report to parents, disciplinary hearings, the newly formed parents' group and the special needs department.

All of the staff of the school – teaching and non-teaching – and those of the governors who were available, spent a training day together analysing the strengths and weaknesses of the school and the opportunities and threats that existed (a SWOT analysis: looking for Strengths, Weaknesses, Opportunities and Threats). This appears to have been a useful session: 'For teachers who hadn't thought about that before, it stopped them being so insular' (Teacher-governor). Governors are also keen to promote the school with parents and within the local community. The newly formed parents' group and membership of the Carnival Committee are examples of these activities: 'If I hear anybody moaning about the school in the Post Office queue, I invite them to visit the school. Trying to get people through the door is the hardest thing' (Parent-governor).

Members of the SMT were aware that they were not as knowledgeable about what was happening in classrooms as they should have been. They linked themselves to departments as line managers and they instituted the practice of seeing every teacher teach at least six times a year. The governors oversee this aspect of the work of the SMT: 'The governor watches me in the line manager role, observing lessons, looking at samples of pupils' work and giving feedback to the head of department' (Deputy head). This was a deliberate decision by the governors and they felt, not unreasonably, that by acting in this way they would be able to assure HMI that they were actively monitoring the work of the school. More recently heads of department have become more involved in this monitoring and some governors have also visited classrooms to observe lessons – this has helped to improve their knowledge and understanding. Staff accept the right of governors to ask questions: 'There are times when practice needs to be questioned' (Teacher-governor). That acceptance, however, is based upon a feeling of partnership and trust: 'Staff now accept governors as part of the common team – they have been supportive in every way' (Teacher-governor); 'Staff don't feel threatened – the governors aren't abrasive' (Teacher-governor).

As part of a support package for the school the LEA appointed, as consultant to the governing body and the SMT, a recently retired head who was currently working at the nearby university. He led team-building sessions for the governing body. The chair believes that such sessions, which address the needs of one school, are more useful than training governors from a number of schools together. It is clear that the consultant's input has been extremely significant: 'He has helped the governing body to work together and helped the staff to see how we could include governors more' (Teacher-governor); 'He made us look at ourselves and gave us confidence; he put the job of the governing body into perspective' (Teacher-governor); 'He focused the governing body much more on the issues' (Governor).

Whatever other effects it may have had, it is clear that the HMI report had a tremendous impact upon the role and work of the governing body of the school. In the special circumstances in which the governors found themselves, they supported the staff and involved themselves in monitoring progress towards the attainment of the targets set out in the post-OFSTED action plan. They have improved their own working practice and enhanced relationships between staff and governors: 'There is definitely a feeling now that governors are part of the school – staff know them better' (Governor). All of this required considerable commitment from the governors.

Issues arising from the vignettes

The three vignettes illustrate very clearly the importance of having a group of committed governors, willing and able to devote time to the school. These governors have to weld themselves into an effective team and to form a real working partnership with the staff, which empowers the governing body. Comments made by staff in the vignettes point to the significance of the latter: without the necessary degree of mutual trust and understanding between governors and staff, the governing body is virtually impotent. Governors need to know and understand their schools; governors who fail in this are at a severe disadvantage. This means that at least some governors must visit the school during the day in order to see the school in action and policy being translated into practice. A well-organised system for monitoring the school's progress towards the achievement of the agreed targets set out in the action plan is essential. The manner in which, and the extent to which, governors are involved in the monitoring will depend upon the circumstances in a particular school. The vignettes also illustrate the potential for support for schools from the LEA; in one case this support included arranging for the secondment of an experienced headteacher to the school and in another for the appointment of a consultant (himself an experienced headteacher) to the governing body.

Leadership in schools is crucial; a former Secretary of State once referred to headteachers as the closest thing available to a magic wand, and although recent thinking points to the significance of leadership *at all levels* in an organisation, there can be no doubt about the importance of high-quality headship. Governors in the schools were given insights from the inspectors' findings as to the quality of the leadership in their schools at both senior and middle management levels. Perhaps unsurprisingly a significant proportion of 'failing' schools – just over one half – have experienced a change of headteacher, either just before or fairly soon after the inspection, as was the case of the school in the Vignette 7.2. There are, of course, many reasons for a head's leadership to falter – incapability or incompetence may be reasons – but whatever the reason the problem of poor or inadequate leadership at all levels has to be dealt with as soon as possible. The governors of the secondary school sought to enhance the management skills of their middle managers by sending ten of them on an MBA course at the nearby university. Issues around the under-performance of classroom teachers have also to be addressed rapidly.

Many governors feel that it is not part of their job to make judgements about the work of professionals (Creese and Bradley 1997) and they therefore rely heavily on professional advice and support in addressing such matters. Initial advice may be sought from the LEA, Diocesan Board or other bodies as appropriate. Most LEA Governor Support Units and Diocesan Boards operate a confidential helpline, whilst the governor-training organisations are also able to offer advice, guidance and support. Governing bodies need access to high-quality advice and guidance so that they are at least aware of the range of options available to them. Interestingly, of those schools that have made considerable progress since their inspection, not all have had a new head or experienced major changes to their staff (as illustrated by Vignette 7.3). In these cases, intensive training and development of existing staff, along with classroom monitoring and a greater awareness of what was required of them (particularly in terms of raising expectations) have been sufficient. The governing body needs to ask questions about what staff training is necessary and to ensure it is adequately funded. The training, motivation and morale of staff have therefore to be addressed and the teachers should see themselves, and indeed be seen, as part of the *solution* to the school's current difficulties, not the source of the *problem*. The governing body has to ensure that plans for improvement are in place, look for outside support and advice where necessary, and back up the headteacher and senior staff.

In the final analysis it is the *teaching staff* who have the greatest influence on the standards achieved by pupils. Governors therefore need to give urgent priority to improvement plans and staffing matters – by both making good appointments and encouraging training – to ensure that the quality of teaching and learning is as high as it can be. Governors may not be able to deliver the educational experience directly to the children but they are able to influence it by ensuring that certain issues are addressed. They need to balance their support of the head's leadership role and responsibility to the pupils against the requirements of employment legislation. Addressing issues of staff under-performance, particularly incompetence, are likely to be both time-consuming and traumatic. Matters are made all the more difficult for governors by the fact that not all of the governing body is able to be kept informed of developments – because of the need for some governors to remain 'untainted', to enable them to serve on appeals committees.

Conclusion

The process of inspection is making it increasingly clear to governing bodies that they have an important responsibility to ensure that their school is effective and well-managed, and governing bodies – not only of 'failing' schools – are reconsidering how they currently perform their duties in the light of the inspector's report. The inspection process has empowered many governing bodies, particularly as they examine their role in relation to the post-OFSTED action plan. For some it has meant, perhaps for the first time, that they have had a meaningful involvement in the school and its decision-making and planning processes. Prior to inspection there may have been an illusion of power but afterwards, given the right conditions and the support of the head, governing bodies have been able to become more involved in their schools, particularly in development and action planning, and in the monitoring of progress. For governors of 'special measure' schools the learning curve is likely to be very steep indeed. Governing bodies of such schools, for a variety of reasons, have often not been operating very effectively or have had a very limited understanding of their role, particularly in relation to the curriculum and helping to raise pupil achievements.

It has been said that being a governor is not the job it once was – schools now need enthusiastic and committed individuals who are prepared to give up their time to perform the role – and research into school governing bodies suggests they can ill afford to have too many 'passengers' on board (Earley 1994). For this reason the period immediately after the inspection may be an opportune time for governors to give consideration to the role and their degree of *commitment* to it. Some of them may decide that the time is right for them to step down to allow more active people to take their place. The LEA or the Diocesan Board could play a most useful role here in encouraging the governing body to consider its roles and responsibilities, and the contribution of individual governors. Fortunately, those schools where considerable progress has been made since their inspections have not been characterised by mass resignations of governors! Neither does it appear that the influx of new or additional governors leads to the formation of polarised governing bodies made up of A-teams and B-teams. Governing bodies of failing schools generally welcomed the appointment of additional governors and saw them as an important source of extra support, expertise and new ideas. Their attitude – which tended to be positive and forward-looking – was one of 'if these individuals will help us to get off the register sooner rather than later then so much the better!'

In their recent review of evidence from just over 200 primary, secondary and special schools under special measures, OFSTED (1997) suggests governors have helped their schools in a number of ways. These include:

- supporting the headteacher to implement change;
- developing the skills to monitor the school's performance;
- organising the governing body more effectively – usually through a series of committees, which have well-defined roles;
- taking an active and high profile interest to support and promote the school;
- tackling difficult issues resolutely, for example, ineffective leadership or teaching, deficit budgets, health and safety issues;
- keeping parents informed about how the school is improving.

(OFSTED 1997: 15)

Governing body reaction and response to inspection, however, has not been uniform. The Institution for School and College Governors (ISCG) notes how governing bodies have reacted very differently – both to the purpose of inspection and to the process: 'In many schools it has been used as an improvement *tool* or yardstick, whereas in others it has been viewed more like a *weapon* inflicting both pain and damage' (Institution for School and College Governors 1996). In many cases inspection has been beneficial because it has forced the governing body to be involved formally and to be called to account. It has also helped to focus their efforts and to unite them against a common outside force. The ISCG believes that OFSTED inspectors are now making more demands on governors to explain how they fulfil their legal responsibilities and that the governing body's main roles 'are being closely examined and dissected'. However, the ISCG states that many are 'neither ready for this scrutiny nor have the language and confidence to articulate what they do' and suggests that 'a realistic approach is needed about what governors should be expected to do for no financial reward'.

Nevertheless, inspection does appear to be encouraging more governing bodies to give serious consideration to how they are performing their duties. Inspection in itself is unlikely to bring about improvements – either in the school or the governing body but, as both Creese (1997) and Gann (1998) have noted, it can act as a powerful stimulus or catalyst for change. A credible and accurate audit of the school and its governing body can be most useful and 'provide powerful ammunition for those governors and teachers who are seeking to change for the better' (Creese 1997).

Inspection and the governing body: questions for consideration

1 Is the governing body aware of its responsibilities?
2 Do governors know what is happening in the school?
3 Do governors have clearly defined roles? Are they efficient and effective?
4 Is the governing body fully involved in the preparation of the action plan? Are governors monitoring and evaluating the implementation of the action plan?
5 Is the governing body monitoring pupils' standards of achievement?

(OFSTED 1997: 29)

Chapter 8

The governing body and parents, pupils and the community

The involvement of parents is potentially one of the biggest challenges we are facing in the next few years. We need to take this on board and manage it rather than reacting to it. We need to push communication (which is good) into involvement.

(Primary school governor)

Introduction

What do we mean when we talk of 'a school'? A school photograph will include the pupils and the teachers, sometimes the non-teaching staff, but where is the governing body? Some of the governors will be members of staff, some will be parents but some of them may have only a tenuous connection with the school. The governors are members of the community as parents, local residents and employers, and the governing body occupies a position on the boundary of the school, partly in the school and partly in the community served by the school. The governing body can act as a bridge between the school and the community, and should be a two-way conduit for communication between them.

Governors are 'the repository of an enormous amount of information, knowledge and understanding of the community' (Gann 1998: 159). Gann suggests that governors can usefully carry out a community audit in which they set out their knowledge under headings such as 'transport', 'voluntary organisations' and 'employment'. Governing bodies can play a very useful role in ensuring that the interests of the community are taken fully into account by the school, for example when considering community use of the school's facilities. When considering such use, the governing body must consider the purposes of community use, the costs to be covered and possible benefits to the school. Some schools are designated as community schools and are particularly well-placed to encourage the idea of education as a life-long activity. Governors, as parents and/or members of the community, can help the school to get its message across to parents and the community. Different ways in which governors have used their knowledge and understanding of the community for the benefit of the school and its pupils have emerged very clearly in our research.

Schools do not exist in isolation; their function is to educate the children of the community which they serve. That community may be small and well-defined, as in the case of a primary school serving a single village, or it may be geographically larger and less clearly delineated. The school building may itself be an important community asset being used for a range of activities in and out of school hours by people other than the pupils and staff of the school. Stoll and Fink (1996) suggest that schools need to reach out to those beyond the school walls in order to bring some cohesion to the fragmentation and mixed messages that many pupils receive. Many schools, especially those designated as community schools, consciously seek to develop their links with the community. In the case of secondary school pupils who leave the school (the school's 'product') may find employment locally or go on to further or higher education. The school is funded by the community and an important aspect of the role of the governing body is to provide a forum in which the staff of the school can render an account of their stewardship. We shall explore this issue further in the next chapter.

Parent-governors are elected to serve as representatives of the parents whose children attend the school. They and the other governors are well placed as members of the local community to act as a channel of communication between the school and that community. The school will have messages that it wishes to address to the community and there may well be messages from the community to the school. We have already seen in Chapter 1 that one of the factors contributing to a climate for improvement is a conscious effort to involve staff, students and the community in the school's policy – and decision-making. Governors are well placed to gather the views of parents and others, and to report them to the school, taking care to ensure that those views include those of the silent majority as well as the vocal minority.

Parents as partners

Research into effective schools shows that parental support and co-operation between home and school has positive effects (Sammons et al. 1995) and there can also be substantial gains in effectiveness when the self-esteem of pupils is raised and when they have an active role in the life of the school. Also, as we have seen in Chapter 1, seeking to involve parents and the wider community in school policies and decision-making will have a beneficial effect upon the climate for school improvement. School buildings should be accessible and welcoming to parents and good communication, both written and verbal, between school and home is essential. Written reports on pupils' progress should be clear, honest and to the point, and homework can be another link in the chain of home–school communication. Some schools have developed 'parents' corners' where parents can sit, read educational literature and talk informally to one another and to teachers – and indeed to governors.

Parents have a considerable contribution to make to their children's education by offering support, encouragement and motivation. Actively involving them and raising their expectations can help to raise standards. All parents possess insights and information about their children that will be of value to the school; and the majority of them, at least, will collaborate with the school in reinforcing its policies and values. They should be aware of the school's targets and those of their child, and what is required for their achievement. Some parents will be able to offer more tangible support, perhaps as helpers in the classroom or on school trips. Some will contribute to fund-raising through the parent–teacher association and some will wish to be involved in the development of the school's policies. The governors, including of course those governors elected by the parents, have a role to play in ensuring that the professionals do not lose sight of the distinctive contribution that parents can make to the school. Governors, for instance by attending meetings of the student council, can also listen to pupils' views and opinions and, when appropriate, seek to see that these are taken into account when school policy is discussed.

Wolfendale (1983) believes that parents have the right to be treated as equal partners, rather than clients, in the education of their children. Clients are passive in the receipt of services, dependent upon expert opinion and peripheral in decision-making. Partners, on the other hand, have equal strengths, equivalent expertise and are able to contribute to as well as receive services and to share the responsibility. Wolfendale (1992) lists a number of premises that should underpin the involvement of parents in schools. These assumptions include the following:

- all parents care about their children's welfare and well-being;
- parents want to co-operate with the school and do what they believe to be in the child's best interests;
- the involvement of parents should include involvement in decision-making and not be merely a matter of the passive receipt of information;
- all parents have the right to be involved and to contribute.

Governors can, where necessary, help to persuade the professionals that parents do have a part to play in the education of their children and that seeking the active involvement of parents will contribute to raising standards and achieving agreed targets.

Vignette 8.1   The governors' Students, Parents and Community Committee in a secondary school

> One of the key things about this school is that we are really seeking lots of new ways of reaching out to parents, to involve them in the teaching process.
> (Teacher)

The staff of a secondary school encourage pupils to take responsibility for their own work and behaviour, and show high expectations of their pupils. The school is also concerned to develop a strong sense of partnership with parents. A newsletter for parents is published regularly and includes items such as 'Meet a pupil' and 'Meet a member of staff', which feature individual pupils and members of staff. Perhaps there might usefully have been a feature entitled 'Meet a governor'! There is an active school council and representatives from the council meet with the governors' Students, Parents and Community Committee from time to time. This committee consists of three governors and three members of staff (including the deputy head and one of the teacher-governors) and meets three or four times a term. Over the past few years issues that have been discussed by the group include:

- student attendance/behaviour/uniform;
- student performance, e.g. homework, revision schedules, exam stress, etc.;
- pastoral care, e.g. social areas for students, racial harassment;
- school organisation, e.g. school day/timings, school size/class size;
- links with parents, e.g. parents' meetings;
- links with business and the community;
- the marketing and promotion of the school.

Vignette 8.2   The governors and head of a primary school seek parental views

The headteacher and governors of a village primary school were keen to obtain the views of parents about the school and their involvement with it. In order to obtain this information the chair of governors interviewed a random sample of parents. Attendance at the meetings for parents to explain the school curriculum had not been encouraging and so the school arranged a series of coffee mornings for parents. The meetings are attended by between twenty and forty parents (predominantly mothers though one or two fathers have attended), and two or three governors. The meetings start at 9.15 a.m. and last for about one hour and a crèche is provided (which is much appreciated). The parents sit around tables in small groups. A range of topics such as school uniform, the school's behaviour policy and the school's sex education programme have been discussed. These meetings provide an opportunity for the headteacher to discuss issues with a group of parents in an informal way. Having governors present enables them not only to become more informed but also to hear parental views. The disadvantage of the timing of the meetings is that working parents are unable to attend. Following the success of the coffee mornings with parents arranged in small groups, a similar format has been used successfully for the annual meeting between governors and parents.

Vignette 8.3   The governors' Pupil Services (Welfare) Committee in a secondary school

This group consists of two governors, the deputy head (pastoral), the teacher with overall responsibility for pastoral care and the teacher-governor. Minutes are taken by a member of the school's administration staff. The governor who chairs the group was herself a pupil at the school and her children attended the school. She is a local magistrate and publican and is well known locally. Recently, the remit of the group has changed from being a formal stage in the school's disciplinary procedures to having more of an advisory and supportive role for pupils and their parents. The group is not now concerned directly with pupil exclusions though the chair does receive notification of any permanent exclusions and would raise any concerns with the head. Pupils and parents can, and do, ask to see the panel on matters such as the quality of school dinners and bullying. Heads of Year are seen on a rota basis by the group throughout the year.

As well as addressing more general issues of pupil welfare and behaviour the group interviews individually pupils whose attendance record gives rise to concern. Pupils are also seen when congratulations are in order: 'We give equal status to good as well as bad' (Governor); 'It is good for children to recognise that people want them to do well' (Teacher-governor). Pupils who are seriously misbehaving are interviewed together with their parents. In these interviews the governors try to be as supportive and positive as possible though they also make their concerns very clear: 'Children get complacent with the staff. We're an unknown quantity. The children are a little wary – they're not sure just what our powers are' (Governor); 'The fact that they aren't teachers makes a difference – they [the governors] have a street cred' (Deputy head, pastoral). When there was an instance of serious bullying in one form, the governors saw the pupils concerned individually, their parents individually, pupils and their parents together and the pupils as a group. As a result of the efforts of the staff and governors the difficulties ceased.

Vignette 8.4   The governors of a primary school work with the headteacher to address issues of concern to the community

One junior (7–11-year-olds) school has just over 300 pupils on roll for almost all of whom English is their second language. The school serves a stable, tightly knit and supportive community in which the three main languages are Gujarati, Punjabi and Urdu. English is not spoken in many of the homes and some written home–school communications are provided in languages other than English, though some parents are not used to reading their own language. A very large proportion of the pupils are Muslim and go to the local mosque after school. Given the nature of the community served by the school there are a number of particular issues facing the staff and governing body. Ideally, all communications from school to parents would be translated into Gujerati, Punjabi and Urdu but this is expensive. Some parents have only a limited grasp of English and so are unable to help their children with homework as much as they might wish to.

One of the issues facing the school, and highlighted in its OFSTED report, is the low attendance rate (the school has almost the worst attendance statistics in the LEA). Not only do parents take their children on extended holidays to India or Pakistan but they also allow them to miss school to attend weddings or religious festivals with their families in other towns, meet relatives arriving or departing at the airport or go shopping. The head was very anxious to enlist the help of the governors in an attempt to convince the parents of the importance of uninterrupted schooling in the primary phase. Accordingly the head met with three governors and an education social worker from the LEA. The governors present felt that the main problem was the attitude of the parents. One of the governors offered to analyse the statistics from the registers in more detail using appropriate computer software. It was hoped that this would give a clearer picture of the nature of the problem and the areas to be targeted.

It was decided to:

- write a letter to all parents (in three languages) setting out the governors' concern about attendance;
- send a follow-up letter from the governors to those parents whose children's attendance gave particular cause for concern;
- enlist the help of the local mosque;
- consider writing articles for the two locally distributed free newspapers;
- follow up more promptly any unexplained absence.

The target was to achieve a 50 per cent reduction in the present absence rate by July 1998.

To provide for the very high proportion of Muslim children there are two assemblies for them each week, with alternative provision being made for the Christian and Hindu pupils. The headteacher takes one assembly each week, another is devoted to presentations devised by the classes in turn and the other to the presentation of certificates etc. One Muslim parent expressed dissatisfaction with these arrangements to the extent that he visited other parents and persuaded them to withdraw their children from the non-Muslim assemblies. The head was very concerned by this because she wished to maintain the school as an integrated community. She enlisted the help of the chair of governors and another governor who is a local councillor (both of them themselves Muslim). The chair wrote to all parents and the councillor visited those who had stated their intention to withdraw their children from assemblies. The head also enlisted the help of the *mufti* from the local mosque who was most helpful and supportive. Eventually only two children ended up being withdrawn, one of them being the daughter of the parent who had originally raised the issue.

Vignette 8.5   The involvement of the governors of a primary school in promoting the school

The governors of a village primary school set up what they termed 'The Positive Promotion Group' whose terms of reference were:

1   To regularly glean for items of interest and prepare them for publication in the local area newspapers.
2   To assemble, collate and display or disseminate photographs or accounts of the school's successes in the local environment.
3   To maintain an archive of school photographs and other materials, and consider how they may be used in the matter of positive promotion.
4   To assist the parent–teacher association in the matter of promoting fund-raising activities, and to be a focus for others wishing to publicise events etc.
5   To consider other ways to promote positively the good work of the school but avoid any competitive or comparative elements that could damage the coherence of the pyramid of schools based upon the local High School.

This group, as its name suggests, is concerned primarily with promoting a positive image of the school in the community and consists of four governors. It is also responsible for the production of the annual governors' report to parents. The governors were keen to make their report more attractive to parents. They instituted a competition in which the pupils were invited to submit designs for the cover of this document. This was so well supported by the children that an additional prize was awarded and some of the artwork was also used in the main body of the report to break up the print. The report included brief pen-portraits of the governors and teachers. An interesting feature were tributes, some in verse, from the pupils to the retiring deputy head. The governors were keen to attract parents to the annual meeting of governors and parents, and hoped that the report would encourage parents to attend. Refreshments were provided before the meeting commenced at 7.30 p.m. and, in order to help parents towards a better understanding of the work of the governing body, there were presentations from representatives of the three working groups that had recently been set up by the governing body: 'This will make the role of the governors come alive in the parents' minds for the first time' (Head).

Issues arising from the vignettes

The five vignettes show governors acting as links between their schools and the community in a wide variety of ways. They illustrate how governors can have direct contact with parents and pupils in addressing a very wide range of issues. The first example shows how governors can be involved in the discussion of issues relating to pupil welfare in their school and how pupils, in this case representatives from the school council, can be given an opportunity to speak directly to governors. When developing the school's strategic plan this group of governors took a broad view of the school's role in the community (see Vignette 4.2). They recognised that it was important that the young people leaving their school should be properly prepared to play an active part in a democratic society. The governors were keen to see that the school plays a full part in addressing the issues facing the community, not only in school hours but outside them as well. Through the operation of their Staff, Students and Community Committee this governing body has provided a forum in which these issues can be discussed and appropriate action planned.

The second vignette illustrates how governors can actively seek the views of parents. Faced with a poor attendance at evening meetings, the school was prepared to be flexible and to arrange meetings at a time that suited more parents. Parents could go on to the meeting immediately after they had left their child at the school and the provision of a crèche accommodated any younger children they might have with them. Parents were invited to contribute their views on a wide range of issues.

It is worth noting that the governors of the secondary school in Vignette 8.3 were at pains to congratulate pupils who had been successful as well as interviewing pupils and/or their parents who were in conflict with the school. The governors were able to reinforce the school's message but were also able to take a slightly more detached stance. Their intervention offered pupils a last chance before exclusion was considered and it was clear that the governors' efforts in this regard were respected and valued by the parents.

The governors of the primary school described in Vignette 8.4 were in a particularly strong position and were able to act as mediators because they themselves were members of the community served by their school. They shared the community's religious and cultural traditions in a way that the teachers could not. By expressing their views as members of the community and as governors of the school they were able to exert considerable influence and to offer support to the headteacher and staff.

The primary school governors described in the final vignette were promoting a positive image of their school in the community and were anxious to enhance communication between governors and parents. They worked hard, as other schools have done, to make the governors' annual report to parents as attractive and readable as possible. It is perhaps unfortunate that the mass of information that governors are required to provide can make the report difficult to digest. Any moves to reduce the amount of detail required are to be welcomed. However, in spite of their best efforts, attendance at the subsequent meeting at which parents could discuss the report was disappointing. The fact that the local football team was entertaining very prestigious visitors that evening may have had an effect! Over the years these meetings have generally been poorly attended, many schools being pleased to see an attendance of parents that reaches double figures (Hinds *et al.* 1992). This may be because parents are being asked to comment upon events that are over and done with; they have read the report and feel that there is little that they can usefully add. Schools that have asked parents to discuss issues of future policy at these meetings have generally had a better attendance. Will the latest inclusion of targets set by the school attract more parents to the AGM?

Conclusion

The vignettes include instances where governors have been able to have a very considerable impact upon their schools. In the case of the primary school described in Vignette 8.4, the intervention of the governors helped to improve attendance rates and eased the tension between parents and school over assemblies. The governors of the secondary school (Vignette 8.3) also helped to increase pupil attendance and improve pupil behaviour in general and in particular to reduce bullying. By contrast with these direct interventions, the governors in Vignettes 8.1 and 8.2 were concerned to involve parents in more general terms and to give them an opportunity to contribute to the school's policy-making. In Vignette 8.1 the governors were also keen to listen to and respond to the views of students. The chair of governors in a primary school had also made a point of attending the student council for the same reasons.

The governors' report to parents and the meeting at which parents have the opportunity to discuss the report with the governors are important links in the chain of accountability (see Chapter 9). Many schools have made great efforts to make the report attractive and readable as their success in the annual competition for these reports run by the *The Times Educational Supplement* shows. Generally, however, attendance at the meetings has been poor in spite of all of the efforts by schools to tempt parents by offering refreshments and/or entertainment. Governors have to continue their efforts and explore, in partnership with the parents, the most fruitful ways of developing communication between them.

Governors' relationships with parents, pupils and the community: questions for consideration

1   How strong are the links between governors and parents, pupils and the wider community? How might they be strengthened?
2   How is the governing body contributing to the development of the educational partnership between the parents and the school?
3   How effective are the annual governors' reports to parents and the subsequent meeting as channels of communication between governors and parents? How might communication be enhanced?
4   How can the governing body contribute to the enhancement of links between the school and the community that it serves?

Chapter 9

Accountability and the governing body

Introduction

The history of the relationship between governors, LEAs and central government is one of change, particularly over the last fifty years. The role and significance of the governing body in the management of the school has changed significantly over the years, from a position of autonomy through subservience to the LEA and back again towards a greater degree of independence. In 1833 Parliament voted the first grant of public funds to education that was conditional upon schools being open to inspection and being administered under an approved scheme of management. Public funding thus demanded accountability, locally through boards of managers and centrally through inspection. LEAs were established as a result of the 1902 Education Act and their position was reinforced by the 1944 Education Act, which laid the foundations of 'the national service locally administered'.

Since State schools educate the community's children and are funded by the tax-payer, it seems only right and proper that schools should be held to account by the community for the education provided. A guide to good governance issued to all heads and chairs in the mid-1990s sees the governing body as 'accountable to those who establish and fund the school and also to parents and the wider community for the way it carries out its functions' (DfEE 1996). The introduction of delegated budgets (LMS) by the Conservative administration in the late 1980s was, in part at least, an attempt to ensure greater accountability and to raise standards. Schools were funded on the number of pupils within them, and it was therefore argued that the more popular, that is the more 'successful', schools would attract more pupils and hence more resources that would enable them to improve still further. Less popular schools would have less money and would therefore either raise their educational standards or 'wither on the vine'. However, no matter how popular a school is, it can only take a fixed number of pupils unless it is in a position to build more accommodation. Increased expression of parental choice may lead to increased levels of dissatisfaction as parents are unable to get their child into the school of their choosing. Indeed, there is increasing evidence that it is the (successful) schools that are doing the choosing rather than the parents (Whitty *et al.* 1998). Parental choice has become parental preference.

In England and Wales, governing bodies, with their elected parent-governors and co-opted representatives of the community, are an important link in the accountability chain. They may be seen as the means through which the producer, the school, is to be made responsive to the consumer, that is the parent – or perhaps more correctly – the child. The governing body can represent (being representative *of*) the community when it calls the school to account for its actions but it also provides a mechanism through which the community may have a voice (being representative *at*) when key policy issues are decided. There are however difficulties in this for the lay governors who have no expertise in the field of education.

The relationship with local and central government

Under the provisions of the 1944 Education Act, LEAs had to ensure that all schools had a Board of Managers (primary) or a Board of Governors (secondary). The majority of the appointments to these Boards were in the hands of the LEA (except in the case of the Aided Schools) who were also to provide Rules of Management and Articles of Government setting out the responsibilities of governors and managers. However, the grouping of one or more schools under a single body of managers or governors was expressly permitted under Section 20 of the Act and Baron and Howell (1974) found that in the boroughs only one-quarter had individual governing bodies for each school; and that even in the shire counties, this proportion rose only to just under a half. They argued that governors and managers were operating on the edge of the network of relationships that make up the educational system. Headteachers and LEA officers saw governors and managers as potentially disruptive and unpredictable, and were concerned to control them as much as possible.

Sallis suggests that the greatest weakness of the 1944 Act was its failure to give any guidance as to the kind of people who were to be appointed as governors or managers: 'Perhaps it was inevitable that managers or governors either became meaningless appendages of the schools or mere tools of the providing authority. ... One thing is certain, they were incapable, as organised in the Sixties, of responding to a new awareness of the importance of parental support ... and the rights of the consumer' (1988: 110). Disenchantment with the system led to the establishment of a Committee of Enquiry in 1975 under the chairmanship of Lord Taylor and their Report, published in 1977, recommended radical changes. Every school should have its own governing body that was to be responsible for the success of the school in every aspect of its work and governors were to do their best to promote communication and good relationships, not only within the school but also between the school and the community that it served. The Committee hoped to encourage the development of a true partnership between the professionals and the lay governors. The members also wished to see equality of representation in the constitution of the governing body with the LEA, the parents, the staff (including the headteacher *ex officio*) and the local community each finding one-quarter of the membership.

The Education (No. 2) Act of 1986 took up the main recommendations of the Taylor Report and produced a radical change in the composition of governing bodies (the term manager disappeared), which effectively ended political control by the LEA. Governors were now required to produce an annual report on their work for parents and to hold a meeting at which that report is discussed. Hardly had the changes introduced by the 1986 Act been digested than it was followed by the 1988 Act: 'While the 1986 Act caused a tremor in schools, the 1988 Education Act brought about an earthquake' (Gann 1998: 20). The role of the LEA was diminished in a number of ways. Control of the school's budget (based upon the number of pupils in the school) was delegated to the governing body. Central government, in the form of the Department for Education and Science (DES), would provide some funding directly to schools for priorities established centrally. Increasingly, LEAs could be by-passed in the decision-making process. Finally, through the introduction of grant-maintained status, schools were given the opportunity of opting out of LEA control altogether. Such schools were to receive their funding direct from the centre, via the newly established Funding Agency for Schools. The governing bodies of these schools have very considerable powers and it is not always clear to whom they are accountable. Legislation passed in 1998 enabled these schools to become 'Foundation' schools with at least some local representation on the governing body.

Are governors representative of the community?

Deem (1992) has pointed out that democracy and accountability imply that those involved in governing schools should include a cross-section of the population. However, it is by no means certain that the composition of governing bodies reflects accurately the communities served by their schools. For instance, successive surveys (e.g. Keys and Fernandes 1990; Earley 1994, Scanlon *et al.* 1999) have found that the majority of governors come from the middle class. There are also issues of gender and race in the make-up of governing bodies although, in the most recent survey, over three-quarters of the respondents felt that their governing body was representative of the community served by the school (Scanlon *et al.* 1999).

Overall, while there are approximately equal numbers of male and female governors (op. cit.), about 60 per cent of the governors in secondary schools are male and, overall, only about one-third of the chairs of governors are female. The appointed LEA and elected parent and teacher governors have the power to co-opt further governors up to a specified limit and when considering co-options, the governors are required to ensure that their governing body reflects a balance of interests. However, Streatfield and Jefferies (1989) found that about two-thirds of all co-opted governors are male, which suggests that ensuring sexual parity on the governing body is not a prime consideration when making co-options. Almost all governing bodies (and certainly all of those in our sample) have set up standing Committees in order to handle their business more efficiently. However, Deem and her co-workers (1992) suggest that Finance Committees, which often wield considerable influence, tend to be dominated by white men and may be unrepresentative of the governing body, or the community, as a whole.

The number of governors from ethnic minorities across the country is around 5 per cent (Scanlon et al. 1999) and this may not always reflect properly the communities served by some schools. The governors from the primary school in Vignette 8.4 were able to mediate so effectively between the school and parents precisely because they themselves were members of the local ethnic community. There may also be a limited representation from the business and industry community (particularly at senior management level) on governing bodies with the largest number of governors from this group serving as parent-governors rather than co-opted governors. Even among those serving as co-opted governors, just over half were co-opted because of their business or industrial associations (Industry in Education 1995).

Accountability

Research conducted into the operation of governing bodies has demonstrated that the reality – what was happening on the ground – was not necessarily the same as envisaged by the legislation. Several studies have shown that changes in the power and influence of the LEA have not been compensated by a corresponding growth in the influence and role of the governing body. Headteachers, perhaps not surprisingly, have tended to step into the vacuum created and are now in a potentially very powerful position (for example, see Levacic 1995; Shearn et al. 1995a, 1995b). The latter research team identified three types of response to the changing situation brought about by the legislation and LMS. There were governing bodies where:

- the headteacher was clearly in charge and made all the significant decisions, either because the governors wanted it that way, did not possess the competence or interest, or because of the tactics used by the head;
- there was a strong working relationship between heads and governors, with both parties clear about the nature of governance and management and contributing to the direction of the school;
- there was disagreement about the boundaries of responsibility and control which often resulted in conflict between the two.

(Shearn et al. 1995a)

The first type of response was found to be the most common and the researchers concluded that the legislation and LMS have resulted in more powerful headteachers and that 'for most schools the governors' role seems to be very limited, sometimes being no more than "supportive" and "advisory"' (Shearn *et al.* 1995a: 187). Rarely were governing bodies involved in issues of *accountability*, in terms of either being accountable to the community served by the school or in being able to 'call the school to account'. In our case studies the heads and chairs of governors reported that they were accountable to parents, school pupils, the community and the LEA. Heads also said that they felt responsible to the governing body, which was in turn seen to represent the interests of the community.

One difficulty for governing bodies is that, until very recently, governors have been heavily reliant on the information given to them by the headteacher. As the chair of governors of a school that, following an OFSTED inspection, had been placed on the register of schools in need of special measures, said: 'I didn't know what I didn't know!' Thomas and Martin (1996) argue for governors to have access to independent sources of information and performance data, and there have been significant moves in this direction in the late 1990s with the introduction of benchmarking and comparative school performance data. There is now an opportunity for a genuine dialogue of accountability in which governors and staff can together discuss information, including comparative data about 'how well we are doing' (see Chapter 5). Thomas and Martin contrast this with situations in which the governors either merely listen to reports prepared by the headteacher and/or staff (accountability by listening) or when governors draw upon their experience or expertise in other fields to question the teachers (accountability by questioning).

Governors, and parents, are now being provided with more and more information about the school's performance, past, present and (via target-setting) future, and the opportunity to compare the achievements of their pupils with those of children in other schools, most importantly, of a similar type. The reports produced by OFSTED inspectors provide governors with an independent 'snap-shot' view of their school (see Chapter 7). The so-called 'league tables' are now well established and educationists are becoming increasingly sophisticated in devising means of measuring the 'value-added' by schools. From spring 1998 schools have had access to benchmarking data (from the QCA) and performance and assessment data or PANDAs (from OFSTED). Many LEAs have also produced comparative data or profiles for schools and governors to use for planning and target-setting (see Chapter 5). From September 1998, governing bodies are charged with the statutory responsibility to ensure the school sets targets in the National Curriculum core subjects (English and Maths) at Key Stage 2 and in public examinations. These targets will have to be made known to parents and progress reported on them in the annual governors' report to parents (DfEE 1997c).

The accountability of senior staff by performance review

Another accountability mechanism is through the rewards offered to senior school staff – a return in some ways to the system of 'payment by results'. When considering a pay increase for the head and deputies, the governors are required to set clear targets and performance indicators though, on the evidence provided by OFSTED inspections, not all governing bodies are doing this: 'Few governing bodies establish and use rigorously clear and relevant performance indicators to help them make justifiable decisions about the salary of the headteacher' (OFSTED 1998, par. 69). The governing bodies involved in our research were also finding this task problematic although it was being tackled.

Heads and deputies are currently paid spot salaries (i.e. non-incremental salaries) that are decided annually by the governing body as part of its pay review. This was introduced by the *School Teachers' Pay and Review Document* (1994), which required governing bodies to undertake a review of heads' and deputies' salaries each September. The governing body has to decide and keep under review what the head and any deputies should be paid. An increase in pay is not permitted unless these targets have been set; they do not necessarily have to be achieved, however, for an increase to be awarded. Similarly, the governing body must approve annually each teacher's position on the pay spine and have, at least in theory, the power to withhold, if necessary, the award of an annual incremental rise.

The School Teachers' Pay and Conditions of Employment (1998) sets out:

> the four criteria to which the relevant body (the governors) is to have regard 'in particular, but not exclusively' in determining the spine point on which the headteacher and any deputy headteachers are to be paid. These are:
>
> - the responsibilities of the post
> - the social, economic and cultural background of the pupils attending the school
> - if the post is difficult to fill
> - whether there has been a sustained high quality of performance of the individual in the light of the performance criteria previously agreed between the governors and the head or deputy.

In relation to the latter point about individual performance, an earlier *aide-mémoire* from the DfEE in 1995 suggested that in annual salary reviews the following indicators should be taken into account by governing bodies:

- examination and test results;
- pupil attendance;

- financial management;
- progress on the implementation of the post-OFSTED action plan.

From September 1997, any discretionary movement in pay could only take place following a performance review. When undertaking such a review previously agreed criteria must be established between heads and deputies and the governing body. There is no requirement to consider pay with a view to a salary increase but if an increase is to be awarded then performance criteria and targets have to be agreed (but not necessarily met). The whole process should be co-ordinated through the appropriate committee of the governing body; there should be enough governors who are not involved in the process to consider an appeal if necessary.

Vignette 9.1   Setting targets and salaries for the head and deputy

In one primary school, the salaries for the head and deputy, and their targets for the coming year, are set by a small committee consisting of four governors including the head. The chair of governors is not a member so that she is available to act in the case of any appeal. Neither the head nor the governors found the negotiations easy: 'It's very hard because I can see both points of view' (Head). The governors were very aware of the difficult position in which the head found herself: 'It's an awkward situation for the head' (Governor). As noted above, the factors that the governors could take into account when awarding a pay increase include an increase in the number of pupils on roll, increased responsibilities, the social and cultural background of the pupils, the head's performance in the post and the need to retain an able and experienced headteacher. The governors did not find it easy to arrive at a figure for the increase and indeed during the discussions the proposed increase rose steadily: 'There's no truly logical way of dealing with this' (Governor).

Matters that arose during the discussion included the fact that some of the class teachers in the school would automatically receive an annual increment of over £1,000 while the head had to negotiate with the governors for an increase that may be less than £500. There was concern to maintain the differential, which is not large in a small school, between class teachers at the top of their pay scale and the headteacher, as well as the differential between the head and deputy. Both the head and the governors are aware of the budgetary constraints that may be severe in small schools: 'We can certainly justify an increase but we have to consider our finances as well' (Governor); 'I'm torn because I know what's in the budget. For seven years I've always put the budget ahead of everything else. Now I have to think of myself' (Head). Finally, it is not clear how closely pay for the head and deputy should be linked specifically to an improvement in pupils' achievements. The corollary might well be that the pay of senior staff would fall if there was a decline in pupils' attainments.

The governors were divided on the issue of how directly any increase in the head's salary should be linked to performance relating to targets. One governor felt that an increase should be awarded for future potential and development rather than for past performance:

> I remain unhappy with linking performance on targets with pay. I feel better at looking back on a year's work well done; I see an increase more as an incentive than as a reward – it's easier to sustain incentive than reward.
>
> (Governor)

However, another governor took a different view: 'We are very happy [with the head's performance]. The targets were difficult and realistic; therefore they could be linked to performance and the head was awarded an increase on that basis.' Increasing pupil numbers was not one of the head's targets but nevertheless the number on roll *had* increased and this might be thought due to the head's leadership, although it could simply be a result of more families moving into the area. Should an increase in pupil numbers be related to the pay of the head and deputy? Do more pupils equal greater responsibility, therefore more pay? A good head is likely to attract more pupils to a school, which brings more money into the budget. How far should this be reflected in the head's salary?

Issues arising from the vignette

Target-setting and performance review in relation to heads' and deputies' salaries has proved problematic for many governing bodies. In order for discretionary movement up the scale to take place, a performance review must occur and this must be based on the review of previously agreed criteria and targets. These should be realistic, understandable and achievable. Without performance criteria and targets, a review cannot be held and the pay of the head or deputy cannot be increased. The reality, however, is that some heads are having their pay increased without proving they have fulfilled the agreed performance criteria (*The Times Educational Supplement*, 9 January 1998). According to a survey conducted for the School Teachers' Review Body (STRB), 28 per cent of heads and deputies who stayed in the same post received at least one additional pay point. But one-third received the additional pay without having their performance reviewed. OFSTED, in their evidence to the STRB, have also questioned governors' abilities to undertake this task effectively. The system clearly needs time to bed down but there has been considerable debate about whether or not governors should be involved in this activity. The issue appears to be – if not governors, then who should have this responsibility? If we must have such a system, then it is argued, in the absence of personnel managers, governors are probably better qualified than any other body (e.g. *The Times Educational Supplement*, 6 December 1996; 17 January 1997). But, as the vignette shows, this responsibility is not without problems. In its 1998 report the STRB refers to the need to provide more training for governors in performance review. It also mentions the possibility of heads' and deputies' salary progression being linked, at least in part, to the achievement of the school's targets for improvement, which, as outlined earlier, all schools and governing bodies are legally required to set (see also Chapter 5).

Governing body accountability

If the teachers are being made more accountable to the community through the governing body, one has also to consider the governing body's accountability to the community. The governing body is being made more accountable to parents and the wider community through the inspection process, which gives attention to the operation of the governors under the 'Management and Administration' part of the inspection Framework (see Chapter 7). However, at present there are some serious limitations to the accountability of governing bodies. Governors, once elected, are not easily deposed before the end of their four-year term of office. They can be removed through not attending three successive meetings (or six months' non-attendance) but generally it is very difficult to remove a 'renegade' or 'maverick' governor. This points to the crucial importance of a proper induction programme for all new governors and for the governing body to spell out clearly what is acceptable and unacceptable behaviour.

As noted earlier, the 1986 Education Act requires that the governing body publish an annual report to parents that explains how the governing body has put into practice its plans for the school during the previous year. It must hold a meeting at least once a year at which parents may discuss the governors' annual report and any other relevant matters, such as the progress made on the points covered in the post-OFSTED action plan and progress made against the targets set. One form of accountability is therefore the governors' annual report and meeting with parents. Anecdotal and research evidence, however (Arden 1988; Hinds et al. 1992), suggests that these meetings are generally very poorly attended and are failing to provide an adequate forum in which the governing body can render account. The schools in the majority of our case studies also reported poor attendance, which was not, however, seen as reflecting parents' lack of interest in the school.

Conclusion: a new model of accountability

The degree to which governing bodies can be perceived as part of the school or the community is likely to vary, with some being seen as an integral part of the school and its management. For others there will be a certain distancing with the governing body still seen very much in terms of an adjunct or 'bolt on' rather than being embedded in the structure of the school and its decision-making processes. We have set out to show throughout this book how some governing bodies are working closely with their schools, being accountable to and accountable for their schools whilst acting as a bridge between the school and the community served by the school.

As has been shown, the nature of the relationship between the various parties – central government, local government, and schools and their governing bodies – has changed over the years. The role of LEAs has waxed and waned, and the most recent legislation may well produce further changes. The need for 'partnership' between the various parties is more important than ever if overall educational standards are to be raised. As the millennium approaches, it may be that the LEA will, once again, play a significant role, particularly in relation to school improvement (Wood 1998) but very much in conjunction with the other stakeholders.

The governor-training organisation, AGIT, has spoken in terms of local partnerships for school improvement as 'a new accountability and a new professionalism' (Martin et al. 1997). A model that locates public accountability within an enhanced partnership between schools and their LEAs (see Figure 9.1) has been proposed and it is suggested that this refocusing 'reflects the maturity of a system of school governance which can be confident in the exercise of accountability by the public for the public' (Martin et al. 1997: 4). The model links accountability to professionalism through the governing body; accountability is the glue binding the partnership together in a spirit of mutual respect and reciprocity. The governing body is therefore seen as playing a key role in raising standards because of its unique position at the interface of the school and the community. It is the link between the headteacher and the professional staff, the LEA, parents and the community, and as such 'a key forum for the mediation and dialogue between all the stakeholders who comprise the local partnership' (Martin et al. 1997: 5). As such governors provide that all-important bridge to the community, operating at times externally to the school and at others being an integral part of the school itself. Schools are accountable to their governors, and the governing body is accountable to the parents, the community and the LEA.

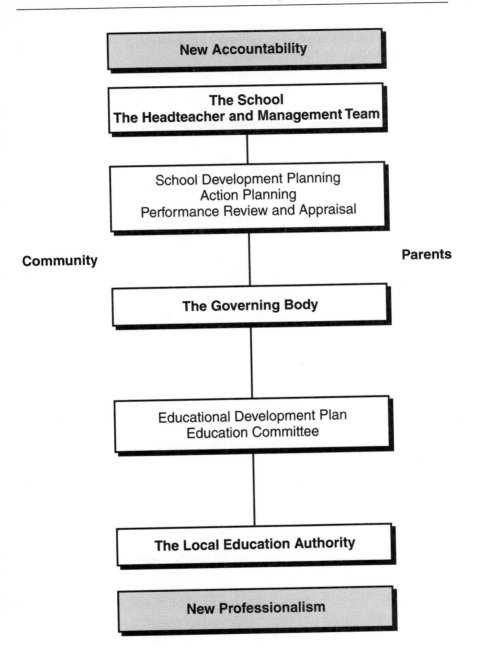

Figure 9.1 A new accountability – a new professionalism: local partnerships for school improvement

Accountability and the governing body: questions for consideration

1   How representative is the governing body of the community served by the school?
2   What needs to be done if the governing body is unrepresentative?
3   By what means is the governing body accountable to the school?
4   By what means is the school accountable to the governing body?
5   By what means is the governing body accountable to the community?
6   Are realistic performance targets being set to help determine heads' and deputy heads' salaries?
7   The annual governors' report to parents and the subsequent meeting are important means of accountability. How might they be made more effective?
8   Is the governing body keeping parents and the community informed about how the school is improving?

Chapter 10

Towards school and governing body improvement

Introduction

In this book we have tried to show how governors, in a wide range of schools and in very different circumstances, have been able to contribute in real terms to improvement, and to the climate for improvement, in their schools. However different their situations, there appear to be a number of factors that are common to all of the schools in our study. All of the governing bodies organised themselves in such a way as to reflect their priorities; all of them delegated much of their work to subgroups. Those committees or working parties were often tasked with very specific roles, some of which were short-term while others were on-going. Often these groups included teachers as well as governors and helped to foster good relationships between them. In every school, the governors were very closely involved in, and very supportive of, the life and work of their schools. Inevitably the amount of time that individual governors could devote to their schools varied according to their personal circumstances but there was a high degree of commitment throughout. Allied to this commitment, and reflective of it, were the close partnerships between governors and staff in all of the schools. Another source of strength was the fact that the governors were representative of the communities that were served by their schools and felt themselves accountable to those communities. We wish, in this closing chapter, to explore some of these common strands in more detail and to highlight the benefits of effective governance.

'We need to be better at targeting the really big issues and giving ourselves time to discuss them' (Primary school governor). This governor suggested, quite rightly, that his governing body needed to plan ahead in order to meet coming changes. He argued that the governors needed to be thinking now about how they were going to address these issues. Several examples of governors 'thinking ahead' have already been featured in this book, including the establishment of a governors' strategic planning group (or Vision Group) and having a governors' Development Plan that sets the governors' targets for the future. The demands made upon schools and their governing bodies will not decrease – indeed they will almost certainly increase! Only those governing bodies that are well-organised and well-led are likely to be able to meet the new challenges.

The governing body as an effective team

We have argued in Chapter 2 that effective governing bodies – those making a difference – are also efficient and operating as well-knit teams; they have clear, agreed and common goals, and the governors are all pulling in the same direction. Common goals may not always be self-evident in the case of a governing body, with its members chosen or elected by different interest groups; and it is therefore important that the governing body as a whole *does* discuss its purposes, aims and objectives, and reaches agreement upon them. Effective teams have sound procedures and good communication systems that are known and understood by all. The role of the chair is crucial in determining the effectiveness of the team; he or she will ensure that every member of the governing body has the opportunity to contribute at meetings, summarise the discussions and make sure that, when required, clear and definite conclusions are reached. The way in which the governing body faces conflict and confronts difficult issues is also important; in an effective team the members support and trust one another and are able to handle conflict openly and constructively, and collective responsibility is maintained.

We have also referred to the benefits of enquiry and reflection. Effective teams regularly review their operation and it should become routine that, just as the work of the school is reviewed in preparing the SDP, so the governing body reviews its operations over the previous year; indeed the Development or Improvement Plan may well include a subsection referring specifically to the governing body. Were the goals that it set itself last year achieved? If not, why not? Would changes in its working methods make it more effective? Is it necessary to consider the recruitment and induction of new governors? What are the targets for the coming year and what training and development for governors will be required?

Reference has also already been made to the fact that many of the governing bodies in the study had arranged training sessions of one sort or another for the whole governing body. These sessions were in addition to the training attended by individual governors and play an important part in building the governors into an effective team. They ranged from a two-day residential weekend for the governors of one of the secondary schools to a two-hour evening session with the staff in a primary school. Where governors and staff work together there are considerable benefits for the partnership between them.

Governors' involvement in the life and work of their schools

> Governors achieve a lot by showing an interest.
>
> (Secondary school teacher)

The reason why governors should know their school well was highlighted by a governor in one school: 'You want to give the head as much support as possible to realise his dreams. You can only do that from a position of strength; you can't do it if you don't know the school.' There was an expectation in many of the schools involved in the project that governors would visit their schools regularly, in some cases at least once a term. Often the governors prepared written reports on these visits that were presented either to the full governing body or to the governors' Curriculum Committee. In many cases governors were linked to specific subject areas and individual governors also took special interest in cross-curricular themes such as the provision for pupils with Special Educational Needs (SEN), or the provision of Information and Communication Technology (ICT) in the school. In some schools, job descriptions were provided for these 'link governors' who were able to take issues, observations and concerns from the staff back to the governing body. Sometimes members of staff with responsibility for different aspects of the curriculum were invited to talk to the governing body about their work and to answer questions. This high level of involvement by the governors was seen as very important by the staff: 'If a governing body is to function as it should, governors must have a good knowledge of the school' (Secondary school teacher).

In addition to visiting classrooms, the governors attended a very wide range of other activities such as plays, concerts and Parent–Teacher Association (PTA) functions. In some of the schools governors attended meetings of the student council. They found it useful to accompany pupils and staff on day trips and residential visits: 'You see how the children behave when the pressure is off. The children have a lot of respect for each other – that's a reflection of the school' (Primary school chair). Many of the governors have, or have had, children in the school and this was thought to enhance the relationship between staff and governors: 'Knowing staff as a parent or helper helps the governor–teacher relationship' (Governor). Governors attended open days held for the parents of prospective pupils and they were sometimes involved in interviews with pupils and parents to discuss serious pupil misbehaviour. The involvement of governors in this way was seen as important in reminding pupils and their parents of the partnership between the governors and the staff. Staff morale was also improved through the involvement of governors.

There were very close relationships between the head and chair of governors that often included the vice-chair: 'The chair and I are talking all the time about the future of the school – it's a trilogy (with the headteacher) – ideas get shared' (Primary school vice-chair); 'The combination of head and chair is the most powerful thing in a school' (Primary school head). The strength of this relation-ship is an important factor in determining the overall effectiveness of the governing body: 'One of the key issues is how the head works with the chair. If there is openness and trust there – a freedom of communication – then this is cascaded down through the staff and governors' (Primary school governor).

The various headteachers' open styles of management contributed consider-ably to the atmosphere of trust between them and their governors: 'The head has a very open style which involves governors' (Primary school chair); 'I don't try to hide anything from the governors. I trust them enough to be honest with them' (Primary school headteacher). However, both headteachers and gover-nors recognise that trust takes time to establish and has to be worked at:

> I've had to prove that what the head tells me in confidence won't go any further. It's a question of building up the trust so that you can believe what you are being told.
>
> (Primary school chair)

> The governors are so supportive of the school and staff that nothing is done which isn't in the school's best interests. The governors are very good at respecting the staff as professionals. One weakness of the governing body is that they trust us so much that they wouldn't dream of making constructive criticism.
>
> (Primary school teacher-governor)

This last comment points up the danger of the relationship between governors and staff becoming too 'cosy'. However, we found that where positive relation-ships between the governors and the staff had been developed, governors could ask questions without appearing critical: 'Questioning at meetings is done in a professional way – there's nothing personal. We don't have heated discussions because openness means that you are part way towards seeing the other point of view' (Primary school head).

Governor–teacher relationships

> It's not 'us' and 'them' – it's 'we' when governors come into school and staff recognise this.
>
> (Primary school head)

> You've got to get the confidence of teachers and pupils.
>
> (Primary school governor)

The importance of fostering the partnership between governors and staff, and the need for the staff to take the lead in this process was clearly recognised in all of the schools in the study:

Getting governors into school and involving them really gets them on board. If they are knowledgeable about the school then they are much more likely to make sound decisions. The school needs to be proactive, inviting governors in, sharing what the expectations are and providing opportunities to develop the partnership.

(Secondary school deputy head)

Governors could also play their part; for instance, in one primary school the governors held one of their three meetings of the year at 4.15 p.m. so that there is an opportunity for the staff to meet with the governors between the end of school and the start of the governors' meeting. In all of the schools involved in the study governors were keen to show their appreciation of the work of the staff and believed that it was important for the staff to have a perception of the governors and senior management team of the school working together in partnership. Governors in general are now less remote and have a better understanding of how their schools function.

The staff in all of the schools appreciated the efforts that the governors had made to get to know the school: 'Governors now pop in and out – they're all very approachable' (A member of the office staff in a primary school); 'They're much more vitally active and knowledgeable now' (Primary school teacher); 'They are very supportive – they put a lot of time into the school and there is a good working relationship between staff and governors' (Secondary school deputy head). Both staff and governors recognise that the governors' role has changed in the past decade:

A governor's role has changed from a rather benevolent side-liner to one which needs some positive input.

(Primary school governor)

In the past the governors have taken a less active role than they do now.

(Primary school teacher)

The governors have got to play a major role in improving the school, having a long-term view of where the school is going. Governors now have far more idea of what is going on in the school than they did, say, five years ago. This makes them more confident.

(Primary school deputy head)

However, both staff and governors are aware that there is a fine line between helpful comment and interference: 'The problem is to express a concern without the teachers feeling that we're being critical' (Governor); 'Teachers must believe that governors are not there to tell them how to teach' (Governor).

The benefits of an effective governing body

The headteachers involved in our research all agreed that there were many benefits in having an effective governing body. It was clear that the advantages to the head and the school that accrued from having a good governing body were many and easily outweighed any extra work that may have been generated as a result of governors' increased responsibilities. Headteachers stated positively that they were now having to explain more fully to lay people what the professionals had too often taken for granted; they were being required to make things more explicit, translate the coded language and jargon of education, and fill in background details so that governors could make informed decisions: 'Because I have to communicate with my governing body, it helps me to analyse and make explicit why I would like to see things changed ... having to explain has made me a better manager' (Head).

A common thread running through the heads' comments was the appreciation of the support they received from their governing bodies. This support was often personal as well as professional. We found governing bodies expressed concern about the health and welfare of their headteachers, and, indeed, of the whole school staff. One headteacher had been away ill in the summer term and on her return the chair ensured that all governing body meetings were completed by 10 p.m. at the latest so that she would not be overtaxed. It was said that good heads needed looking after! Support from the governing body can also go some way to help remove the feeling of isolation that is commonly recognised as being an integral part of headship. The expectations laid on the 'school leader' can be very great and these pressures, along with the notion that 'the buck stops here', mean that the job is often very stressful. Being a head was seen as a lonely job and there were not always many sources of support where heads could talk openly and frankly about issues and problems. Heads were able to do this with their governors, particularly chairs and vice-chairs of governors. The support that the governing body was able to offer the head was said to be crucially important because 'it's lonely at the top' and 'you can be very isolated as a headteacher'.

The governing bodies involved in our research were conscious that headship could be a very lonely and highly pressured job. Headteachers were grateful for the opportunity to be able to share the responsibility for the running of the school with their governors who, they found, were prepared to listen to them and provide them with support when the governors felt this was necessary and justified. This was particularly true of the relationship between the headteacher and the chair of governors. A secondary school headteacher believed that this relationship affected how the whole school operated and, therefore, it was crucial that this relationship 'should be right'. For this headteacher the chair provided 'an ear to bash, a shoulder to cry on and someone to bounce ideas off'. According to the heads, chairs of governors required certain key qualities: they needed to be accessible, keen and interested. One head frequently off-loaded his problems on the chair and used her as a sounding board: 'She is very sharp and with-it. That's really useful; it helps me to crystallise my thinking' (Head). The good relationship between the headteacher and the chair was often cemented by mutual respect and a common view of the way the school should be run and on education in general.

Support from the governing body was sometimes described by the heads in terms of 'protection'. The governing body could take away some of the responsibility, the worry and the criticisms: 'The protection for the headteacher is because a lot of the conversation is corporate and the main dealings of the school are through the committees.' Another head commented:

> It is useful to have a body rather than individuals making agreements and decisions – it both protects and strengthens the school. I personally find it easier to deal with situations when I know there is a clear policy made by the governing body and I know I have implemented that policy.

Most governing bodies recognised the importance of their role as critical friend to the headteacher and to the school. One chair defined a critical friend as one who 'asks the questions in order to get the best answers'. Headteachers realised searching questions could sometimes be painful. One school's governing body was prepared to say to the headteacher: 'We asked you to do this! Why haven't you done it? We are prepared to smack botties!' (Chair). The opposite could be true, as in the case of the headteacher who was felt by the governors to be moving ahead too fast. Her governing body restrained her and said, 'Hang on a minute!' Headteachers also commented that governing bodies could help to clarify issues by posing probing questions or requiring more detailed answers. For example, one headteacher had drafted a person specification and one of her governors queried whether or not she had in fact meant what she had written. She realised on reflection that it was not what she had intended and changed it. The head was grateful that this error had been spotted.

One of the most important attributes of a governing body was said to be that it is largely composed of individuals who bring different perspectives to the headteacher and the school: 'a knowledge of the world outside, of where education is going, of the world of work and unemployment' (Head). Governors felt they 'added in areas of expertise and avenues that were not necessarily open to the school' (Head). One headteacher found that the governing body gave her the opportunity to learn from different people with different backgrounds. Another realised that sometimes the professionals were too close to the issues or had trammelled vision: 'you simply can't see the wood for the trees'. Having a group of people with a variety of skills and experience was an added resource for headteachers. This could enhance their role and make their jobs easier.

Overall headteachers were beginning more fully to appreciate the benefits of having a good chair and an effective governing body in what could, otherwise, be a lonely and, at times, vulnerable position. They could find sympathy and understanding, as well as challenge and stimulus, from a body of hard-working and committed lay-people who had the best interests of the school at heart. Headteachers could take comfort from the comment of the headteacher who said: 'As I'm accountable to everybody they [the governing body] take some of that responsibility off me because it's ultimately the governing body that carries the responsibility for the school.' Heads reported being able to sleep more easily, assured that any decision taken was a collective one.

The nature of headship is such that the more assistance made available to the head the better. A governor trainer likened the role of the head to a plate spinner. Heads, it was suggested:

> are attempting to do so many things – it's a multifaceted post and the nature of the job is such that at any one point some of the plates are being wound up and really going and others are tottering on the edge of disaster – and where an effective governing body comes into play is if the head uses the governing body well, you've got an extra few pairs of hands to keep the plates spinning.
>
> (LEA Governor Trainer Co-ordinator)

The heads involved in our research regarded their governing bodies as resources to be used and developed in a similar way to that of the staff of the school. If a head was not developing his or her staff then questions would surely be asked. Was the same not equally true of the governing body? Governors were seen as 'adding value' by calling heads to account and by questioning, where necessary, decisions that had been made. The value of the governing body was that it offered a range of different perspectives and prevented schools from becoming insular.

Conclusion

It is sometimes said that schools get the governing bodies they deserve. Whether this is true or not is difficult to say. What we can say with some conviction, however, is that governing bodies when they are operating well are capable of 'making a difference' to a school and in particular can be invaluable to the head. In our case studies governors and staff believed that the governing body made a significant contribution to the life and work of the school, seeing it as an important resource, offering support and encouragement, acting as a sounding board, providing specific (non-educational) skills and perspectives, while also helping to give direction to the school. The governing bodies involved in our research were characterised by commitment, co-operation and professionalism.

School improvement is currently high on both political and educational agendas. The role of governors in school improvement was first highlighted in *Improving Schools* (OFSTED 1994b) and the White Paper, *Excellence in Schools*

(DfEE 1997f). The subsequent 1998 Education Acts state clearly that the purpose of governing bodies is to help to provide the best possible education for the pupils in their schools. It is clear from our research that governing bodies *can* contribute to improvement in their schools but evidence from the reports of OFSTED inspections suggests that a proportion are failing to do so. A key issue for the future will be the empowerment of all governing bodies so that they can contribute effectively to school improvement. Perhaps inevitably, some schools are better served at present by their governing bodies than others. If all governing bodies are to become truly effective and to have a significant impact upon the work of their schools, then change is essential. This change will not necessarily be easy and some form of catalyst, such as a new headteacher or chair of governors, an OFSTED inspection or a training event, may be required to bring about this change. Hopefully, this research will make its own small contribution to both governing body and school improvement by helping governors not only to understand more fully just how much they can contribute but also what forms that contribution might take. If, through our research, we help to make governing bodies more efficient and effective so that they can raise the standards and enhance the quality of the education received by the pupils in their schools, then our work will have been worthwhile. We wish you the best of luck in your endeavours!

Appendix
The schools involved in the study

Almondbury High School, Huddersfield, Kirklees

A school for 11–16-year-olds that serves an area of mixed private and council housing though its intake is significantly skewed towards the lower end of the ability range. There are currently 735 pupils on roll, a staff of 42 and 16 governors. The school sees itself as a community school with 1,000 adults coming into the school during a typical week for adult education courses.

Barstable School, Basildon, Essex

A Grant-Maintained (GM) comprehensive school for 11–16-year-olds; there are currently just over 1,000 pupils on roll. The school's intake is skewed towards the lower end of the ability range, with over 50 per cent of 11-year-old entrants having reading ages two or more years below their chronological ages. There are 62 staff and 17 governors.

Chapel Road School, Attleborough, Norfolk

A special school situated in the small market town of Attleborough, drawing pupils from a very wide area of south-west Norfolk. There are currently 59 pupils with severe learning difficulties on roll with an age range of 4 to 19 years. There are 7 teachers plus the head, 16 full-time teacher assistants (TAs) and 2 part-time TAs. There are 9 governors.

Croft Junior School, Nuneaton, Warwickshire

A junior school located just outside the town centre with a catchment area consisting predominantly of council housing. There are just over 300 pupils on roll and the intake is significantly skewed towards the lower end of the ability range. There are 12.5 teachers and 14 governors with a parent about to be co-opted on to the governing body.

Crowfoot County Primary School, Beccles, Suffolk

The school's catchment area is mixed private and council housing. There are currently 300 children on roll plus a nursery class and an area special class; nearly two-thirds of the children have significantly delayed language development on entry to the school. There are 15 members of the teaching staff and 16 governors.

Dalton Junior School, Huddersfield, Kirklees

A mixed school for 7–11-year-olds serving an area of mixed private and council housing that, at the time the research was undertaken, was on the list of schools needing special measures to improve. However, the school is popular with local parents and currently has 277 children on roll. There are 9 full-time members of the teaching staff (including the headteacher) and 2 more teachers operate a job-share to cover one class. There are 12 governors. There is a unit for visually impaired children within the school.

Felsted County Primary School, Essex

Felsted is a relatively small village with a mixture of private and council housing. There are 151 pupils on roll at the school, which plays an important part in the life of the village and is housed in a mixture of Victorian and modern buildings. There are 7 members of the teaching staff including the headteacher and 12 governors.

Green Dragon Infant and Junior School, Hounslow, London

This infants (Reception, Years 1–2) and junior school (Years 3–7), built in the mid-1970s, serves a richly diverse community in the poorest ward in the borough. Many children live in high-rise tower blocks under a flight path to Heathrow airport and nearly 45 per cent of them are entitled to free school meals. A total of nearly 450 pupils are on roll, a figure which is rising but not stable as families, including some refugees, are rehoused in other parts of the borough. There is a growing but small number of pupils from private housing and more advantageous home backgrounds. Attainment on entry varies and about 20 per cent are from ethnic minorities. There are 2 heads and 18 teachers but only the one governing body, which consists of 15 governors.

Grundisburgh County Primary School, Suffolk

This village school, which moved into a new building in 1989, and currently has 145 pupils on roll. There are six full-time members of the teaching staff including the head (who has responsibility for a class) and twelve governors.

Hyrstmount Junior School, Dewsbury, Kirklees

A school with just over 300 pupils, ages 7 to 11, on roll, for almost all of whom English is their second language. A very large proportion of the pupils are Muslim. In addition to the 12 class teachers, there are 6 language development teachers, 3 bilingual support workers and 2 special needs teachers. The governing body consists of 12 governors and reflects the racial mix of the local community.

Kirkheaton Junior and Infant School, Kirklees

Kirkheaton is a moorland village near Huddersfield. There has been a considerable amount of building in the village in recent years and the junior and infant school is housed in a modern open-plan building. There are currently 375 pupils on roll, with 13 staff and 14 governors.

Leeside Junior, Infant and Nursery School, Heckmondwike, Kirklees

The school opened in 1995 in a converted secondary modern school following reorganisation of the schools in the area. It serves an area of mixed council and private housing and there are currently 260 pupils on roll, with 10 teachers and 12 governors.

Mandeville High School, Aylesbury, Buckinghamshire

A mixed comprehensive high school for 11–16-year-olds in a market town serving a mixed catchment area with council and private housing. Nearly 550 students on roll with 60 in the sixth form. There are 33 members of the teaching staff and currently 17 governors.

Marlborough School, St Albans, Hertfordshire

A GM mixed comprehensive school for 11–18-year-olds on the western side of St Albans with some 620 pupils on roll including around 120 in the sixth form; the roll is currently rising. There are 45 members of the teaching staff and 18 governors.

Mary Linwood School, Leicester

A mixed comprehensive school for 11–16-year-olds on the south-western side of Leicester that is on the list of schools in need of special measures to improve. The school serves one of the most run-down areas of the city with high unemployment and a high crime rate locally. Pupils enter the school with reading ages up to two years behind their chronological ages. There are 400 pupils on roll, 34 members of the teaching staff and currently 16 governors.

Nascot Wood Junior School, Watford, Hertfordshire

A school for 7–11-year-olds sharing a site and a governing body with an infant school, situated in an attractive suburb. There are about 250 pupils on roll with a teaching staff of 9.5. The joint governing body consists of 16 governors together with the headteacher of the infant school.

R.A. Butler Junior School, Saffron Walden, Essex

The school, which shares a site with an infant school for 4–7-year-olds, became GM in April 1995. The governing bodies of the infant and junior schools meet as one. There are 12 members of staff in the junior school and 18 governors.

Sandy Lane Junior School, Bracknell, Berkshire

A junior school on the outskirts of Bracknell serving a mixed catchment area of both private and public housing. There are 250 pupils on roll with the intake skewed towards the lower end of the ability range. There are 11.5 members of the teaching staff and 11 governors.

St Alban's High School, Ipswich, Suffolk

A Roman Catholic aided mixed comprehensive school for 11–16-year-olds, which draws children not only from Ipswich but also from a wide area around the town. There are at present 500 pupils on roll, 35 members of the teaching staff and 20 governors. The school was nominated in Her Majesty's Chief Inspector's Report for 1996/97 for its outstanding performance.

St Mary's Primary School, Banbury, Oxfordshire

A primary Church of England school located in a small village a few miles from the market town of Banbury. The school has 52 children in the nursery and over 230 in the main school. There are ten teachers, excluding the head, and twelve governors.

St Matthew's Aided Primary School, Ipswich, Suffolk

A school on a somewhat cramped site in the centre of the town, which currently has 321 pupils on roll (a significant proportion of whom are Black). The school has been over-subscribed in recent years. There are 12.8 full-time equivalent teachers including the head and 14 governors.

Stratford High School, Stratford, Warwickshire

Stratford comprehensive is a mixed high school (a former secondary modern) with over 1,100 students aged between 11 and 18. The students are predominantly from less affluent backgrounds and tend towards the lower end of the ability range. There are 60 members of the teaching staff and 19 governors (there has been a vacancy for an LEA governor for over a year).

Temple Cowley Middle School, Cowley, Oxfordshire

This middle school caters for pupils aged between 9 and 13 years, and serves a suburb of Oxford whose main employer is a well-known car manufacturer. The 560 pupils on roll, of which 20 per cent are from ethnic minorities, are from less than affluent backgrounds. The intake is skewed towards the lower end of the ability range. There are 24.5 teachers on staff and 15 governors (the governing body currently has 4 vacancies, including the 2 teacher-governors).

Bibliography

Arden, J. (1988) 'A survey of Annual Parents' Meetings by the London Diocesan Board for Schools' in P. Earley (ed.) *Governors' Reports and Annual Parents' Meetings: The 1986 Education Act and Beyond*, Slough: NFER.

Audit Commission/OFSTED (1995) *Lessons in Teamwork*, London: HMSO.

Baginsky, M., Baker, L. and Cleave, S. (1991) *Towards Effective Partnerships in School Governance*, Slough: NFER.

Baron, G. and Howell, D. (1974) *The Management and Governance of Schools*, London: Athlone Press.

Bradley, H. (1991) *Staff Development*, London: Falmer Press.

Bullock, A. and Thomas, H. (1997) *Schools at the Centre? A Study of Decentralisation*, London: Routledge.

Costa, A.L. and Kallick, B. (1993) 'Through the lens of a critical friend', *Educational Leadership* 51(2): 49–51.

Creese, M.J. (1993) 'Equal partners? A study of relationships between governors and teachers', in G. Wallace (ed.) *Local Management, Central Control: Schools in the Market Place*, Bournemouth: Hyde Publications.

—— (1994) *Inspecting the Governors*, Ipswich: School Governance and Management Development.

—— (1995) *Effective Governors, Effective Schools: Developing the Partnership*, London: David Fulton.

—— (1997) *Effective Governance: The Evidence from OFSTED*, Ipswich: School Management and Governance Development.

—— (1998) 'The strategic role of governors in school improvement', in D. Middlewood and J. Lumby (eds) *Managing Strategy in Schools and Colleges*, London: Paul Chapman.

Creese, M. and Bradley, H. (1997) 'School improvement and the role of governors: Findings from a pilot project', *School Leadership and Management* 17(1): 105–15.

Cuckle, P., Dunford, J., Hodgson, J. and Broadhead, P. (1998) 'Governor involvement in development planning; From tea parties to working parties', *School Leadership and Management* 18(1): 19–34.

Dean, J. (1985) *Managing the Secondary School*, London: Croom Helm.

Deem, R. (1992) 'Governing by gender? School governing bodies after the Education Reform Act', in P. Abbott and C. Wallace (eds) *Gender, Power and Sexuality*, Basingstoke: Macmillan.

Deem, R., Brehony, K. and Heath, S. (1995) *Active Citizenship and the Governing of Schools*, Buckingham: Open University Press.

DES (1991) *Development Planning: A Practical Guide*, London: DES.

DFE/BIS/OFSTED (1995) *Governing Bodies and Effective Schools*, London: DFE.

DfEE (1996) *Guidance on Good Governance*, London: DfEE.

—— (1997a) *School Governors: A Guide to the Law*, London: HMSO.

—— (1997b) *Investors in People and School Self-improvement*, London: DfEE.

—— (1997c) *Setting Targets for Pupil Achievement: Guidance for Governors*, London: DfEE.

—— (1997d) *From Targets to Action*, London: DfEE.

—— (1997e) *The Road to Success: Four Case Studies of Schools which No Longer Require Special Measures*, London: DfEE.

—— (1997f) *Excellence in Schools*, London: HMSO.

—— (1997g) *Excellence for All Children*, London: HMSO.

Earley, P. (1994) *School Governing Bodies: Making Progress?*, Slough: NFER.

—— (1997) 'External inspections, "failing schools" and the role of governing bodies', *School Leadership and Management* 17(3): 387–400.

—— (1998) 'Governing bodies and school inspection: Potential for empowerment?', in P. Earley (ed.) *School Improvement after Inspection? School and LEA Responses*, London: Paul Chapman.

Esp, D. and Saran, R. (eds) (1995) *Effective Governors for Effective Schools*, London: Pitman.

Everard, K.B. and Morris, G. (1996) *Effective School Management*, London: Harper Row.

Ferguson, N., Earley, P., Fidler, B. and Ouston, J. (1999) *The Inspection of Primary Schools: Factors Associated with School Development, Final Report to the Nuffield Foundation*, London: Nuffield Foundation/Institute of Education.

Fullan, M. (1991) *The New Meaning of Educational Change*, London: Cassell.

—— (1992) 'Causes/processes of implementation and continuation', in N. Bennett, M. Crawford and C. Riches (eds) *Managing Change in Education*, London: Paul Chapman.

Gann, N. (1998) *Improving School Governance: How Better Governors Make Better Schools*, London: Falmer Press.

Harris, A., Jamieson, I. and Russ, J. (1996) *School Effectiveness and School Improvement: A Practical Guide*, London: Pitman.

Hinds, T., Martin, J., Ranson, S. and Rutherford, D. (1992) *The Annual Parents' Meeting: Towards a Shared Understanding*, School of Education: University of Birmingham.

Holt, A. and Hinds, T. (1994) *The New School Governor*, London: Kogan Page.

Hopkins, D. (1994) 'Yellow Brick Road', *Managing Schools Today* 3(6), March: 14–17.

Hopkins, D., West, M. and Ainscow, M. (1996) *Improving the Quality of Education for All: Progress and Challenge*, London: David Fulton.

Industry in Education (1995) *All their Tomorrows: The Business of Governing*, London: Industry in Education.

Institution for School and College Governors (1996) *Inspection – a Weapon or a Tool, a Post-mortem or a Health Check?*, The Governors' Analysis, Occasional Papers No. 4, London: ISCG.

Keys, W. and Fernandes, C. (1990) *A Survey of School Governing Bodies*, Slough: NFER.

Koontz, H. and O'Donnell, C. (1968) *Essentials of Management*, London: McGraw-Hill.

Levacic, R. (1995) *Local Management of Schools*, Buckingham: Open University Press.

Martin, J., Earley, P., Holt, A., Hesketh, J., Pounce, M. and Sheriton, J. (1997) 'School governing bodies: From policy to practice', paper resulting from an invitational seminar, Institute of Education, London, September.

Matthews, P. and Smith, G. (1995) 'OFSTED: inspecting schools and improvement through inspection', *Cambridge Journal of Education*, vol. 25, pp. 23–4

Mortimore, P. (1991) 'The nature and findings of school effectiveness research in the primary sector', in S. Riddell and S. Brown (eds) *School Effectiveness Research: Its Messages for School Improvement*, London: HMSO.

Mortimore, P., Sammons, P., Ecob, R. and Stoll, L. (1988) *School Matters: The Junior Years*, Wells: Open Books.

OCEA Partnership (1997) *Governors Monitoring for School Self Improvement*, Old Woodhouse, Leicestershire: OCEA.

O'Connor, M. (1996) 'The OFSTED experience: A governors' eye view', in J. Ouston, B. Fidler and P. Earley (eds) *OFSTED Inspections: The Early Experience*, London: David Fulton.

OFSTED (1994a) *Handbook for Inspections*, London: OFSTED.

—— (1994b) *Improving Schools*, London: HMSO.

—— (1997) *From Failure to Success*, London: OFSTED.

—— (1998a) *School Evaluation Matters*, London: OFSTED.

—— (1998b) *The Annual Report of Her Majesty's Chief Inspector of Schools, 1996/97*, London: HMSO.

Ouston, J., Fidler, B. and Earley, P. (1996) 'Secondary schools' responses to OFSTED inspection', in J. Ouston, P. Earley, and B. Fidler (eds) (1996) *OFSTED Inspections: The Early Experience*, London: David Fulton.

Oxfordshire LEA (1998) *The Effective Governing Body Exercise Manual*, Oxford: Oxfordshire LEA.

Reid, K., Hopkins, D. and Holly, P. (1987) *Towards the Effective School*, Oxford: Blackwell.

Rutter, M., Maughan, B., Mortimore, P. and Ouston, J. (1979) *Fifteen Thousand Hours: Secondary Schools and their Effects on Children*, London: Open Books.

Sallis, J. (1988) *Schools, Parents and Governors: A New Approach to Accountability*, London: Routledge.

Sammons, P., Hillman, J. and Mortimore, P. (1995) *Key Characteristics of Effective Schools: A Review of School Effectiveness Research*, London: Institute of Education, University of London.

Scanlon, M., Earley, P. and Evans, J. (1999) *Improving the Effectiveness of School Governing Bodies*, London: DfEE.

School Teachers' Review Body (1998) *Seventh Report*, London: HMSO.

Sexton, S. (1987) *Our Schools: A Radical Policy*, Warlingham: Institute of Economic Affairs.

Shearn, D., Broadbent, J., Laughlin, R. and Willig-Atherton, H. (1995a) 'The changing face of school governor responsibilities: A mismatch between Government intention and actuality?', *School Organisation* 15(2): 175–88.

—— (1995b) 'Headteachers, governors and local management of schools', in G. Wallace (ed.) *Schools, Markets and Management*, Bournemouth: Hyde Publications.

Stiles, C. (1996) *School Governors and Inspection*, (2nd edition), Coventry: AGIT.

Stoll, L. and Fink, D. (1996) *Changing our Schools*, Buckingham: Open University Press.

Streatfield, D. and Jefferies, G. (1989) *Reconstitution of Governing Bodies: Survey 2*, Slough: NFER.

Thomas, H. and Martin, J. (1996) *Managing Resources for School Improvement: Creating a Cost-effective School*, London: Routledge.

Van Velzen, W., Miles, M., Ekholm, M., Hameyer, U. and Robin, D. (eds) (1985) *Making School Improvement Work: A Conceptual Guide to Practice*, Leuven: ACCO.

Walters, J. and Richardson, C. (1997) *Governing Schools through Policy*, London: Lemos and Crane.

Whitty, G., Power, S. and Halpin, D. (1998) *Devolution and Choice in Education*, Milton Keynes: Open University Press.

Wolfendale, S. (1983) *Parental Participation in Children's Development and Education*, London: Gordon and Breach Science Publishers.

—— (1992) *Empowering Parents and Teachers: Working for Children*, London: Cassell.

Wood, M. (1998) 'Partners in pursuit of quality: LEA support for school improvement after inspection', in P. Earley (ed.) *School Improvement after Inspection: School and LEA Responses*, London: Paul Chapman.

Index